A New Owner's
GUIDE TO
BERNESE
MOUNTAIN DOGS

JG-169

Overleaf: Adult Bernese Mountain Dog owned by Patti Morgan.

Opposite page: Adult Bernese Mountain Dog owned by Maria Wright.

The Publisher wishes to acknowledge the following owners of the dogs in this book, including: Normand Claude, Amy Christiansen, Karen Desiderio, Stephanie Flynn, Diane Harris, Tracy Hopper, Kim Ivie, Linda Klim, Patti Morgan, Lilian Ostermiller, Holly Partigue, Mary Troll, and Maria Wright.

Photo Credits:
Bishop Photography, 91
Paulette Braun, 13, 48
Amy Christiansen, 8, 11, 15, 17, 19, 22, 24, 25, 26, 27, 29, 32, 33, 35, 36, 37, 39, 45, 47, 51, 54, 64, 66, 67, 68, 69, 71, 75, 79, 82, 101, 104, 105, 107, 109, 110, 118, 126, 136, 143, 144, 147, 154
Stephanie Flynn, 21
Isabelle Francais, 31, 52, 55, 57, 61, 62, 63, 70, 74, 77, 78, 80, 84, 87, 92, 97, 99, 100, 112, 113, 117, 120, 127, 132, 137, 139, 141, 145, 148, 153
Dianne Harris, 14, 60, 115, 123
Tracie Hopper, 83, 85, 94, 151
Kim Ivie, 18, 125
Kemp, 88
Linda Klim, 43, 59, 131, 140, 157
Adrienne Rescinio, 30, 41, 73
Karen Taylor, 129
Mary Troll, 9, 10, 23, 28, 44

The author acknowledges the contribution of Judy Iby to the following chapters: Health Care, Sport of Purebred Dogs, Identification and Finding the Lost Dog, Traveling with Your Dog, and Behavior and Canine Communication.

A New Owner's
Guide to
Bernese Mountain
Dogs

Amy Christiansen

T.F.H. Publications, Inc.
One TFH Plaza
Third and Union Avenues
Neptune City, NJ 07753

This book has been published with the intent to provide accurate and authoritative information in regard to the subject matter within. While every precaution has been taken in preparation of this book, the publisher and author assume no responsibility for errors or omissions. Neither is any liability assumed for damages resulting from the use of the information herein.

Library of Congress Cataloging-in-Publication Data
Christiansen, Amy.
A new owner's guide to Bernese mountain dogs / Amy Christiansen.
p. cm.
Includes index.
ISBN 0-7938-2818-X (alk. paper)
1. Bernese mountain dog. I. Title
SF429.B47C57 2004
636.73--dc22
2004001448

www.tfh.com

ABOUT THE AUTHOR

Amy Christiansen grew up with the family's Norwegian Elkhounds, and dogs remained an important part of her life from that time on. However, Amy did not meet her first Bernese Mountain Dog until she was 16 years old, at which time she was working for a veterinarian in Illinois.

In 1991, she acquired her first Berner, Kollin, a 14-week old puppy that was to become Ch. Kollin Von Kieletstar. Since then, strict selectivity has been the keyword at Diamond Creek—with only 42 puppies registered under the name in the ensuing 14 years. Conformation champions, point winners, and a Versatility Dog title holder are among them.

Amy maintains active membership in Alaska's Bernese Mountain Dog Club and has also been a member of the Bernese Mountain Dog Club of America.

Space and time restrictions limit Amy's breeding program, but her degree in animal science and her background as a licensed veterinary technician provide the Diamond Creek Berners with the best care available. Those who own a Diamond Creek Berner, now and in the future, can be assured of all the mental and physical soundness that the breed is capable of having.

Contents

2004 Edition

Lovable and sweet, the Bernese Mountain Dog has many admirers.

The Berner's furry coat and distinctive markings are characteristic of the breed.

**The Berner's easygoing nature
makes him a great playmate for
gentle children.**

**The hardworking Bernese Mountain
Dog is happiest when given a job to
perform.**

The Bernese Mountain Dog enjoys spending time in the outdoors.

The Bernese Mountain Dog reflects many of the wolf's characteristics, such as his territorial instinct, communal spirit, and fierce bravery.

HISTORY and Origin of the Bernese Mountain Dog

ANCIENT HISTORY

The Fédération Cynologique Internationale (FCI) is the canine authority that represents the majority of European and Latin American dog-showing countries of the world. The organization recognizes all the breeds registered in each of the countries it oversees, the total of which numbers well over 400. What comes as a surprise to many is that all of these breeds, regardless of size, shape, or color, trace back to one common ancestor—*Canis lupus*, the wolf.

The road from wolf-in-the-wild to "man's best friend," *Canis familiaris*, is as long and fascinating as it is laden with widely varying explanations. There does seem to be universal agreement in one thing, however, and that is that the wolves that were able to assist man in easing his struggle to survive were the most highly prized.

Human ingenuity deserves a good part of the credit for the selective process that produced dogs that excelled in some but not all of the traits that had been passed down from their lupine

The Bernese Mountain Dog was originally developed in the farming communities of Berne and was referred to by the natives of the area as the Durbachler.

9

Versatile and obedient, the Bernese Mountain Dog thrived on serving the Swiss dairy farmer, whether herding, cart pulling, or guarding his home and family.

ancestors. The undesirable characteristics that could have been inherited were all but nullified. A perfect example of this is seen in how the wolf's territorial instinct, communal spirit, and bravery are reflected in the character of the Bernese Mountain Dog.

Humans, however, can't take all the credit for the changes that transpired during this wolf-to-dog transition. The unique ability of the wolf to adapt to its environment both physically and mentally had created different wolf families with their own distinct characteristics, giving humans more to work with.

When the Mongoloid people migrated westward into Europe, their dogs, the Mastiff-type descendants of the rugged Tibetan wolves, went with them. The migrants dispersed themselves throughout the important mountain ranges of Europe stretching from east to west across Asia and Europe. Environment and the specific needs of the people developed their dogs into separate and distinct types.

THE BERNESE IN SWITZERLAND

Professor H. Kraemer of Berne, Switzerland, has done extensive study of Switzerland's indigenous dog breeds. He believes several types of dogs descended from these Tibetan Mastiffs and that they have existed in his country for at least 2,500 to 3,000 years.

Switzerland's mountainous terrain permitted isolated areas to develop breeds uninterrupted by outside influence for thousands of years, which, of course, resulted in dogs exceptionally consistent in appearance and temperament. One of the types developed in the farming communities of Berne was the Berner-sennenhund (Bernese Mountain Dog), but it was referred to by the natives of that area as the Durbachler.

Early outside influence of any sort on the Berner-sennenhunde remains a point of contention among historians. Some firmly believe that blood of the Mastiffs developed in Southern Europe was introduced when the Roman legions brought their large and fierce Molossian dogs to help them guard the Alpine passes. Others disagree with the possibility of these influences, totally rejecting the idea that dogs traveled with the Roman armies at all. The controversy remains to be resolved.

Nevertheless, the adaptable "dairyman's dog," as the Bernese Mountain Dog was often called, thrived because he was happy to serve his Swiss dairy farmer owner in so many ways. His duties were herding, cart pulling, or guarding home and family, depending on

In 1904, the Bernese Mountain Dog made his first appearance at a dog show at the International Swiss Kennel Club event held in Berne.

the time of day or what the farmer needed at the moment. Versatile was, in a word, what a Berner had to be.

The Bernese Mountain Dog made his first appearance at a dog show at the International Swiss Kennel Club event held in Berne in 1904. There were seven entries, and the dogs drew a great deal of interest—so much so that not much time elapsed before the breed was entered into the Swiss Stud Book.

By 1907, the Schweizerische Durbachler Klub (later Berner Sennenhunde Club) was founded to protect and preserve the breed. Professor Albert Heim, a noted geologist, was judge of the event. Heim was the club's patriarch, and credit must be given to him not only for the Bernese Mountain Dog's status as the national dog of Switzerland, but also for the appearance of the breed as we know it today.

Only three years after the first Berne show, interest in the breed as a show dog had accelerated to the point that the show held in Burgdorf resulted in an entry of over 100 Berners. Professor Heim was again called upon to judge and make comments on the state of the breed.

Notwithstanding disagreement on influences in the breed's early history, there is common agreement and recorded documentation that, for reasons of hybrid vigor and temperament, it became necessary to make an outcross to the solid black Newfoundland in the late 1940s. Carefully documented steps and back crosses were made, enabling the supervised breedings to maintain the desired characteristics of the Berner while what was undesirable was eliminated with the Newfoundland influence.

In just four years and three generations, the Berner's distinctive markings were recaptured, and the improvements in conformation and temperament were successfully set. In fact, the third generation was so successful it produced a male, Alex v. Angstorf, who went on to achieve international titles in the ring and exert influence on the breed throughout the world.

The Bernese Mountain Dog in America

The first Berners arrived in America in the first years of the 20th century. They were the Swiss registered pair, Donna von der Rothohe and her mate Poincare von Sumiswald. Unfortunately, farmer-importer Isaac Schiess' request to have the breed accepted

The Bernese Mountain Dog made his first appearance in the United States in the early 20th century.

A hard worker and amiable companion, the Bernese Mountain Dog was officially admitted to the AKC stud book as a member of the Working Group in 1937.

and registered by the American Kennel Club (AKC) fell on deaf ears. Neither the pairs documented Swiss ancestry nor the Donna and Poincare's US-born litter whelped in 1926 served to alter the AKC's decision.

Ten years later, Glen Shadow of Louisiana also imported a pair of Berners from Europe. His enthusiasm for the breed knew no bounds, and he exerted his considerable influence on the AKC to recognize the breed. Thus, on April 12, 1937 the Bernese Mountain Dog was admitted to the stud book of the AKC as a full-fledged member of the Working Group.

Shadow remained the sole breeder or owner of AKC-registered Berners in America until 1949, when a few more were imported, but no breeding programs were implemented. The breed was at a standstill for the best part of a decade.

In 1959, Nelly Frey produced a litter of puppies out of her female Lory v. Sunnehuebeli, sired by Banz v.d. Kuhweid. The successful mating produced Aya of Verlap, which, under the guidance and ownership of her owners, became the first Berner to gain an obedience degree of Companion Dog.

Mrs. Bea Knight of Drain, Oregon, a highly successful breeder of St. Bernards, took up the cause of the Bernese Mountain Dog and, through her breeding efforts, the first US champions were produced. They were Sanctuary Woods Black Knight, owned by Roberta Subin, and Ch. Sanctuary Woods Black Lancer, retained by Knight. Ch. Sanctuary Woods Gordo, the first Berner to win a Group First in America, was also bred by Bea Knight at Sanctuary Wood.

What the Bernese Mountain Dog lacked in numbers (there were only 43 registered in 1968) was made up for by the enthusiasm of

Responsible and caring Bernese Mountain Dog breeders have made tremendous efforts to ensure that their dogs end up in only the best homes.

those who owned the breed. Carol Pyle and several other West Coast fanciers gathered at the Golden Gate Kennel Club show in January of 1968 and formed the beginnings of what was to become the Bernese Mountain Dog Club of America (BMDCA) in 1972.

The BMDCA held its first championship specialty show in March of 1976 in Harrisburg, Pennsylvania, with the Best of Breed award going to Dr. Mary Dawson's female, Ch. Zyta v. Nesselacker.

Ch. Alphorn's Copyright of Echo, bred and owned by Dr. and Mrs. D. G. Johnson, entered the breed's history books as the '70s came to a close by becoming the first Berner to win an all-breed Best in Show in the US.

Those who champion the cause of their beloved breed have made no effort to make the Bernese Mountain Dog a fad breed. They are firmly convinced that no finer breed exists when it is in the hands of the proper owner, but dedicated breeders exert every effort to make sure that their dogs end up only in the proper hands.

Glen Shadow's original pair were the only Berners registered by the AKC in 1937, and that number was repeated with an odd exception of one or two on through to the mid '60s when interest took a gentle turn upward with 31 registered in 1966.

Nearly 200 Berners were registered in 1972, and interest in the breed rose slowly and steadily from that point on throughout the 1990s. In 1999, the Bernese Mountain Dog ranked No. 51 on the list of 150 breeds registered by the AKC, with 2,567 dogs registered. By 2002, the Bernese Mountain Dog had become the 51st most popular breed in over 2,500 doge registered—and the breed's popularity just seems to keep increasing.

CHARACTERISTICS of the Bernese Mountain Dog

All puppies are cuddly and cute. The Bernese Mountain Dog baby is beguiling beyond words, with his adoring eyes, spectacular markings, and compact little body. Berner puppies have a special teddy bear charm that is hard to resist.

There is nothing more adorable than a litter of Berner puppies, nestled together sound asleep, one on top of the other. But in addition to appearing irresistible and innocent, a Berner puppy is a living, breathing, and very mischievous creature that is entirely dependent upon his owner for everything once he leaves his mother and littermates. Furthermore, the innocent and dependent little Berner puppy that can be held comfortably on your lap when you take him home from the breeder grows by leaps and bounds and quickly becomes a very large and somewhat gawky adolescent.

Buying a dog, especially a Berner puppy, before someone is absolutely sure they want to make that commitment, can be a serious mistake. The prospective dog owner must clearly understand the

The Bernese Mountain Dog puppy is known for his distinctive markings, adoring eyes, and compact body.

Wise and dependable, the Bernese Mountain Dog takes his role as guardian and family companion very seriously. "Kollin" and Haily enjoy relaxing in the grass.

amount of time and work involved in the ownership of any dog. A large breed like the Berner has its own special considerations, which must be added to those of any standard or toy-sized dog. Failure to understand the extent of commitment involved in dog care is one of the primary reasons there are so many unwanted canines that end their lives in animal shelters.

Before anyone contemplates the purchase of a dog, there are some very important conditions that must be considered. One of the first questions that must be answered is whether or not the person who will ultimately be responsible for the dog's care and well-being actually wants a dog. If the prospective dog owner lives alone, all he or she needs to do is be sure that there is a strong desire to make the necessary commitment dog ownership entails. In the case of family households, however, it is vital that the person who will ultimately be responsible for the dog's care really wants a dog. This is a task that cannot be left to "just someone" in the family. There has to be a "designated doer!" In most households, mothers—even working mothers—somehow always seem to end up with the additional responsibility of caring for the family pets. Although mothers are also out in the workplace, they all too often are involuntarily saddled with the additional chores of feeding and walking the dog and trips to the veterinary hospital with what was supposed to be a family project.

Teaching your Berner puppy every household rule that he is expected to obey from the start will help prevent behavioral problems from occurring.

Pets are a wonderful way of teaching children responsibility, but anyone who knows children knows that the enthusiasm that inspires them to promise anything in order to have a new puppy may be totally forgotten tomorrow. Who will take care of the puppy once the novelty wears off? Does that person want a dog?

Desire to own a dog aside, does the lifestyle of the family actually provide for responsible dog ownership? If the entire family is away from home from early morning to late at night, who will provide for all of a puppy's needs? Feeding, exercise, outdoor access, and the like cannot be provided if no one is home.

Another important factor to consider is whether or not the breed of dog you are interested in is suitable for the person or the family with which it will be living. Some breeds can handle the rough and tumble play of young children and some cannot. Even the Berner puppy can be unintentionally harmed by a child who hasn't been properly schooled in puppy care. On the other hand, a dog like the rapidly growing Bernese Mountain Dog youngster is so unaccustomed to his constantly increasing size as a puppy that he could unintentionally injure an infant or toddler.

Then, too, there is the matter of grooming. A luxuriously-coated dog is certainly beautiful to behold, but all that hair takes care. In the case of Berners, they shed their coats twice a year where they live— in the home. Owning a vacuum cleaner and using it daily is a necessary reality in the ownership of a Bernese Mountain Dog.

Remember, also, that as brainy as the new dog's breed might be reputed to be, he must be taught every household rule that he is expected to observe. Some dogs catch on more quickly than others, and puppies are just as inclined to forget or disregard lessons as young human children.

CASE FOR THE PUREBRED DOG

As previously mentioned, all puppies are cute, but not all puppies grow up to be particularly attractive adults. What is considered beautiful by one person is not necessarily seen as attractive by another. It is almost impossible to determine what a mixed-breed puppy will look like as an adult. Nor will it be possible to determine if the mixed-breed puppy's temperament is suitable for the person or family who wishes to own him. If the puppy grows up to be too big or too active for the owner, what then will happen to him?

The multi-purpose Bernese Mountain Dog needs to feel like he is an integral part of the family. Involving your Berner in fun activities, like taking a hike in the mountains, keeps him occupied and active.

Size and temperament can vary to a degree, even within a purebred dog. Nevertheless, selective breeding over many generations has produced breeds like the Berner that give the would-be owner reasonable assurance of what the puppy will look and act like as an adult. Points of attractiveness completely aside, this predictability is more important than one might think.

A person who wants a dog to go along on those morning jogs or long distance runs is not going to be particularly happy with a lethargic or short-legged breed. Nor is the fastidious housekeeper, whose picture of the ideal dog is one that lies quietly at the feet of his master by the hour and never sheds, going to be particularly happy with a huge, shaggy dog or one with a temperament reminiscent of a hurricane.

Purebred puppies will grow up to look like their adult relatives, and by and large, they will behave pretty much like the rest of their family. Any dog, mixed breed or not, has the potential to be a loving companion. However, a purebred dog offers reasonable assurance that he will not only suit the owner's lifestyle, but the person's esthetic demands as well.

Who Should Own a Bernese Mountain Dog?

The Bernese Mountain Dog is a multi-purpose dog. He is a wise and dependable working dog. For the family, he fulfills the traditional role as a companion and guardian to adults, as well as to children, and he eagerly enjoys participating in whatever the family is doing.

A working couple can also make a good home for a Bernese Mountain Dog, provided there is outdoor space for him when they are away at work. When they are at home, the dog should not be left outside but included, whenever possible, in evening and weekend activities. A Berner needs to feel like he is a full-fledged member of the family.

Provisions must be made for the Berner puppy when the family is not at home. Never leave a puppy or teenager loose in the house or unattended at any time. Youngsters can get bored, and if left alone inside a home or apartment, they may end up chewing or getting into things that you do not want them to. Berners are equally adaptable to farm life or apartment dwelling as long as walks in the fresh air are part of the daily routine.

A securely fenced yard is the best place for your Berner when you are not home. Sturdy fencing is recommended, and it must be at least 5 to 6 feet high. It is also important to walk along your fence

The intelligent Berner needs plenty of mental and physical stimulation. Before deciding on a Bernese Mountain Dog, make sure that you can provide him with the proper socialization necessary for a healthy and happy life.

The Bernese Mountain Dog strives to please his owner and revels in his family's company, whether they are indoors or out.

and make sure there are no holes in it or gaps between the fence and the ground.

Access to the whole yard is important when you are there with your Berner. However, if you enjoy gardening, flowers, and shrubs, leaving an attractive garden in your puppy's care is not going to make you happy. Keeping the puppy in a fenced dog run that is tucked away on the side of the house or at the end of the garden when he is outdoors alone is a better idea. A 10- by 40-foot space is adequate for a run, but a larger one is better yet. This, too, should be enclosed with fencing of the proper height. Small-sized gravel several inches deep will keep the Berner clean. A nice, large dog house located at one end is needed to protect him from the elements. Never chain or tie a Berner out and leave him alone. It is inhumane and can lead to aggressive behavior.

Despite the appearance that he is an ideal outdoor dog, the Berner thrives on maintaining close contact with his special people, wherever they are, indoors or out. Do not make the mistake of thinking you can stash a Berner away in his run or yard and forget about him. A Berner would rather spend the day in the back seat of your car or van traveling along from place to place than endure an entire day without you.

THE QUESTION OF SIZE

One of the most frequently asked questions of a Berner owner is, "How much does he weigh?" Above mid-size but not huge would probably best capture the average Berner's size. A fully mature male measures an average of 25-27 ½ inches at the top of the shoulder, while his sister might measure in a couple of inches less.

It is difficult to determine the Berner's weight in any exact amount in that a male at the bottom of the size range might weigh nearly the same or possibly even less than his sister, who is at the top of the size range. Suffice it to say that the weight of most Berners falls somewhere between 75 and 110 pounds.

It isn't absolutely necessary to dash out and buy a station wagon or mini-van to transport your Berner, but it might give you both a more comfortable ride. A full-grown Berner occupies the same space as the average pre-teen child, so take that into consideration when it's time to buy that new car—a sports car might not be the ideal choice.

It's important that you can offer your Berner the proper living accommodations. Before making your final purchase, it's a good idea to research the breed's background, such as its expected weight and height.

Choosing a Bernese Mountain Dog means choosing a new best friend and loyal companion. The bright and eager Berner is a happy addition to any household.

A good socialization program and obedience classes that begin in puppyhood can do nothing but enhance the wonderful personality and character a Bernese Mountain Dog is born with. Excursions to the grocery store, the school yard, and the park all contribute to your dog becoming a good canine citizen.

If you are the type of person who enjoys having a buddy to take long leisurely hikes with, the Berner is an ideal companion. Berners aren't racing thoroughbreds or performance jumpers. Think more along the lines of a big, gentle draft horse and you will have a better sense of your Berner's exercise needs. Traveling at a sensible pace, your Berner could easily accompany you on a coast-to-coast hike.

CHARACTER OF THE BERNESE MOUNTAIN DOG

Bernese Mountain Dogs are first and foremost companions, capable of bonding to their owners like no other breed. Berners live what I call a "we" existence: "Where are we going?" "What will we be doing today?"

Hard working and willing to please, the Bernese Mountain Dog is happiest when he is given a job to do.

Your Berner puppy will move into your life and demand to be a huge part of it. Berner ownership is more like adopting a new family member than it is buying a dog. A Berner doesn't like to lose physical contact with those he loves and finds his owner's foot an ideal place to maintain that contact. After all, if you're sitting on your loved one's foot, he or she can't get too far away!

The Berner is bright, eager, and willing to learn. Although he's far from aggressive, he has a great deal of self-confidence and seems to have a great sense of good judgment that he puts to use in protecting his home and family. A Berner has an incredible sense of humor and appreciates an owner who has one too.

Berner puppies love the world, and that is exactly as it should be. As adults, they like to know who they're dealing with and need a little time and distance to do so. Once they have decided someone is acceptable, they seldom forget that decision. In fact, many decide frequent visitors are no longer guests, but members of their family.

A long history of usefulness and hard work demands that the Berner has more to do in life than lie around and smell the daises. If your Berner doesn't have a real job, it will be up to you to put all that eagerness and ability to good use. This is an extremely versatile breed that is ready, willing, and able to perform in many capacities. The Berner will take to obedience work like the proverbial duck to water and is just as accomplished at things

Bernese Mountain Dogs enjoy the world around them and are very eager to explore their surroundings.

Proper socialization is an essential part of your Berner puppy's development. Allowing him the opportunity to meet strangers will enable him to become a sound and stable member of the canine community.

like agility and serving as a therapy dog in children's hospitals and homes for the aged.

A Bernese Mountain Dog arrives in your home with a built-in love for children and is usually as patient with them as the day is long. My male, Howdy, adores an eight-year old friend who visits us with her mother. Since Howdy is the only playmate available, he gets his little friend's full attention—playing dress-up, tea parties, the whole bit. He loves every minute of it and participates fully like the perfect gentleman he is capable of being.

With that said, no dog should be made to tolerate abusive children. Before bringing a new dog into your home, the children need to be told how to take care of the newcomer and how they must behave around the dog. This is true whether the new arrival is a puppy or an adult.

When you are out walking your Berner puppy, you will find he will attract a lot of attention. For most, Bernese Mountain Dogs are not an everyday occurrence, and therefore, total strangers will come up and want to ask about your "beautifully marked" dog and pet him. There could be nothing better for your Berner. Meeting strangers and learning to be calm and behave himself around them is an important part of being a sound and stable member of the breed.

In describing the characteristics of the Berner, please don't get the impression this is a "cookie cutter" breed. It is important not to generalize, because each Berner has his own likes and dislikes, response rate, and manner in which he expresses himself.

SELECTING the Right Bernese Mountain Dog for You

O nce the prospective Berner owner satisfactorily answers all the questions relating to responsible ownership, he or she will undoubtedly want to rush out and purchase a puppy immediately. Take care—please do not act in haste! Not only is a sound and stable temperament of paramount importance in a large breed of this kind, but there are also a number of problems that can and do exist that good breeders are concerned with. Berners have a good many health problems—many of them orthopedic in nature. The breed has its share of cancer problems, and there are seizure disorders, as well as a good many allergies.

Your Berner will be living with you as close to ten years as your good care and his careful breeding permit. You will undoubtedly want the dog you live with for that length of time to be one you will enjoy.

It is extremely important in this breed that your dog is purchased from a breeder who has earned a reputation over the years for consistently producing dogs that are mentally and physically sound.

Responsible breeders care about their puppies' well-beings and do their best to ensure them long and healthy lives.

Be prepared to answer breeders' questions concerning your lifestyle and living conditions. They want to ensure that their puppies go to stable, loving, and permanent homes.

Unfortunately, the buyer must beware in that there are always those who are ready and willing to exploit a breed for financial gain, with no thought given to its health or welfare or to the homes in which the dogs will be living.

The only way a breeder can earn a reputation for producing quality animals is through a well-thought-out breeding program in which rigid selectivity and testing is imposed. Selective breeding is aimed at maintaining the virtues of a breed and doing one's utmost to eliminate genetic weaknesses. This process is time-consuming and costly. Therefore, responsible Berner breeders protect their investment by providing the utmost in prenatal care for their brood matrons and maximum care and nutrition for the resulting offspring. Once the puppies arrive, the knowledgeable breeder initiates a thorough socialization process. Concerned breeders not only keep their puppies, or adults for that matter, until exactly the right homes are found, they also demand, by contract, that the dogs be returned to them in the event that the situation does not work out. The relationship with this kind of breeder does not end when the buyer walks out the door with his or her puppy—the association continues for the life of the dog. You'll find these breeders do not let puppies go to new homes at Christmas or major holidays or that they be given as gifts without meeting and talking to the prospective new owners. They will never push or pressure you to buy a puppy.

Allow the breeder to help you choose the right puppy for you. A breeder knows each puppy's personality far better than your brief visits might allow you to determine and will be much better at making a suitable match.

WHERE TO LOOK FOR A BREEDER

Governing kennel clubs in different countries of the world maintain lists of local breed clubs and breeders that can lead a prospective dog buyer to responsible breeders of quality stock. If you are not sure of where to contact a respected breeder in your area, contact your local kennel club for recommendations.

The buyer should look for cleanliness in both the dogs and the areas in which the dogs are kept. Cleanliness is the first clue that tells you how much the breeder cares about the dogs he or she owns.

It is extremely important that the buyer knows the character and quality of not only the puppy's parents, but the grandparents as well. Good temperament and good health are inherited, and if the

When visiting a breeder's kennel, make sure that both the dogs and the facilities are clean and well kept.

31

puppy's ancestors are not sound in these respects, there is not much likelihood that they will produce offspring that are. Good breeders will be able to answer any and all questions you should be·asking about these important matters.

Never buy a Berner from anyone who has no knowledge of the puppy's parents or what kind of care a puppy has been given from birth to the time you see him. Even the most well-intentioned owner of a pet shop has no idea how the puppies he or she offers were raised. The pet shop owner is only the middleman. The Bernese Club of America forbids any of its members from selling to pet shops or brokers.

Find a breeder who is honest and has only the intention of placing his or her dogs in the best of homes. When you find your new friend for life, love him and treat him as if he was bred to be part of your family.

A Breeder Checklist

You will find that the Bernese Mountain Dog breeders who are most highly respected and most often recommended in their breed have the following characteristics in common:

1. They never breed their females on first heat, nor do they breed at every heat.

A good breeder will be able to answer questions about the parents and grandparents of your prospective puppy. Their overall health and temperaments will indicate what your Berner will look and act like as an adult.

There are many factors that contribute to a pet's happiness, such as a healthy living environment, good care, and unconditional love.

2. They breed only dogs that are structurally sound and certified by the appropriate authority for being so.

3. They breed only animals of sound temperament.

4. They have spay/neuter contracts or do early spay/neuter before placing puppies.

5. They do their utmost to place the right puppy with the right owner. All puppies do not have the same personality, any more than all humans do.

6. They do not place puppies before eight weeks of age.

7. They require orthopedic evaluations done on all puppies sold by two-and-a-half years of age.

8. They are always available to help and answer questions for new owners.

9. They belong to Bernese Mountain Dog Club of America and/or regional breed or all-breed clubs.

10. They follow the code of ethics of their national club.

A Word About Rescue

Thus far, the breed is fortunate that very few Berners are ever found roaming the streets or in shelters. However, occasionally there are Bernese Mountain Dogs that people can no longer keep. There can be very legitimate reasons such as moving, divorce, allergies, family difficulties, or dog behavior problems.

People involved in rescue take the dogs that need to be rehomed and find out as much as they can about the background of the dog. They do a complete evaluation and then place the dog in a suitable home. Rescue dogs can be any age, from a young puppy to a much older dog.

All responsible Berner breeders take their puppies back for rehoming at any age and this way are able to keep the rescue problem to a minimum. Good breeders would never allow a Berner to be in need. They help by taking in rescue dogs, whether the dogs are of their breeding or not. Others refer potential Berner owners to rescue groups or make donations to rescue funds.

HEALTH CONCERNS

There is every possibility that a reputable breeder resides in your area who will not only be able to provide the right Berner for you, but also will have both parents of the puppy on the premises. This gives you an opportunity to see first-hand what kind of dogs are in the background of the puppy you are considering. Good breeders are always willing to have you see their dogs and to inspect the facility in which the dogs were raised. These breeders will also be able to discuss problems that exist in the breed with you and how they deal with these problems.

The following health issues are presented here so that you will be aware of just how much care, concern, and testing a legitimate breeder's stock undergoes before an individual dog is deemed suitable enough to be included in a breeding program. Don't misunderstand—the following neither indicates a breeder will have any one of these specific problems in their line, nor does it mean that testing can or has entirely eliminated any or all of the problems.

The following discusses the health concerns breeders have and that a good breeder is happy to discuss with you.

Bloat

While bloat (gastric torsion) is not actually known to be an inherited problem, it does occur in the large, deep-chested breeds like the Bernese Mountain Dog with enough regularity to warrant considering it an associated condition if nothing else. Little is known about the actual cause of bloat. Many theories have been offered, but none have actually been proven. This often fatal condition seems to occur frequently at night, after the dog has had

You can help prevent your Berner from experiencing bloat by not letting him exercise immediately after eating and feeding him smaller meals.

a large meal, ingested a great deal of water, and then exercised strenuously.

Symptoms can range from a severe attack of gas to death. It can occur so suddenly and swiftly that only immediate attention by a veterinarian experienced in dealing with the condition will save your dog's life.

Simply described, bloat causes the stomach to rotate so that both ends are closed off. The food contained in the stomach ferments but gasses cannot escape, thereby causing the stomach to swell greatly, pressuring the entire diaphragm, and consequently leading to extreme cardiac and respiratory complications. The affected dog is in extreme pain, and death can follow very quickly unless the gas is released through surgery.

There are three generally accepted tips to aid in the avoidance of bloat:

1. Feed two smaller meals each day as opposed to one large meal.
2. Add water to dry food.
3. Limit exercise following a meal.

Canine Elbow Dysplasia (CED)

There are three issues relative to CED—ununited anconeal process, fragmented caronoid process, and osteochondritis dissecans. An affected dog may suffer from one to all three in one or both elbows. The exact causes are not yet known, although

Maintaining your Bernese Mountain Dog's health should be a top priority. Providing him with the proper vet care, exercise, and nutrition will keep him healthy and content.

heredity is a factor in rapidly growing breeds. Trauma to the joint is also a factor.

Radiographic evaluation of the elbows is required by most breeders, as some affected dogs never show clinical signs. The degree to which CED takes place causes lameness varying from an occasional limp to a chronic condition. If any elbow disorder is suspected, it is extremely important to seek advice from a veterinarian who has had experience in dealing with canine elbow dysplasia so that the correct diagnosis can be made.

Ununited Anconeal Process

In a young dog, the anconeal process is cartilage that gradually turns to bone and unites with the rest of the ulna (one of the two bones of the forearm). This occurs at approximately four to six months. When this union fails, it is called ununited anconeal process (UAP). UAP leads to degenerative joint disease (DJO) due to the instability of the joint.

Breeding only the best-quality dogs ensures that the Bernese Mountain Dog will stay free of hereditary diseases.

Fragmented Coronoid Process

As with the anconeal process, this begins as cartilage and gradually turns to bone as it unites with the ulna. Failure of that fusion to occur is known as fragmented coronoid process (FCP). Expect development of DJO in this case as well.

Osteochondritis Dissecans

Osteochondritis dissecans (OCD) is a condition in which the cartilage lining the bone surfaces in the shoulder joint and elbow or stifle and hock joints are weakened to the point where it cracks, allowing the bone beneath it to become exposed and painful. The degree to which it takes place causes lameness varying from an occasional limp to a chronic condition.

Hip Dysplasia (HD)

Hip dysplasia is common, but seems to be radiologic in incidence rather than clinical in appearance. Simply put, hip dysplasia is a failure of the head of the femur to fit snugly into the acetabulum, with resulting degrees of lameness and faulty movement. The inheritance of the defect is polygenic, which means there is no simple answer to the elimination of the problem. Breeders routinely x-ray their breeding stock and breed only from superior animals that have been graded in the categories deemed acceptable for breeding.

While it is important that both the sire and dam have been x-rayed and cleared for breeding, it is just as important that littermates, grandparents, their littermates, and so on, have been x-rayed and their history known. Family selection is at least as important as individual selection in the case of polygenic diseases. Asking a breeder the hip status on the parents of the litter and about the incidence of hip dysplasia in their line would be an important question for any breeder of the Bernese Mountain Dog.

As a pet owner, it is important for you to know that individual dogs whose hips might not rate above a grade of "fair" can lead a long and normal life without any sign of lameness. They should never be bred, however.

Osteosarcoma

Cancer of the bone is not entirely uncommon in the Bernese Mountain Dog, and as we now know human medicine, tendencies toward certain types of cancer are known to be more prevalent in some families than others. Osteosarcoma manifests itself in the Berner by a persistent lameness of a leg, and a malignant tumor will develop. Another good question for a Berner breeder is, "Have you had occurrences of osteosarcoma, or any other cancers, in your line?"

Patella Luxation

This condition is also commonly referred to as "slipping stifles." It is an abnormality of the stifle or knee joint leading to dislocation of the kneecap (patella). Normally, the kneecap is located in a groove at the lower end of the thighbone. It is held in this position by strong elastic ligaments. If the groove is insufficiently developed, the kneecap will leave its normal position and "slip" to one side or the other of the track in which it is normally held.

The dog may exhibit an intermittent but persistent limp or have difficulty straightening out the knee. In some cases the dog may experience pain. Treatment may require surgery.

Clear, bright eyes are signs of good health. Consult your veterinarian if your Berner's eyes appear irritated.

Cruciate Ligament Injury

Two of the ligaments that support the knee joint cross over the center of the joint in a cruciform shape. They provide stability in this area of weak connection. Heavyweight dogs that are forced to flex their joints excessively by jumping or sudden turning can rupture the anterior ligament of the pair.

An initial sign of this damage is slight limping, but sensitivity increases with more exercise and can evolve to the point at which no weight can be put on the leg at all. Rest and stabilizing the joint can relieve the condition entirely, although corrective surgery is prescribed in some cases.

Entropion

Entropion is a condition in which the eyelids are turned inward so that the eyelashes constantly rub against and irritate the eyeball itself. Untreated, it can severely damage vision. A surgical procedure can fully correct the condition.

Surgery to correct entropion prohibits dogs from being shown in American Kennel Club (AKC) conformation dog shows (the rules bar any dog that has had surgery that has altered the dog's appearance). Entropion is a painful eye condition, and there should be no question that a humane owner would choose corrective surgery over a show career. The AKC's stipulation applies only to conformation show events and does not restrict the dog from competing in any AKC performance events.

Ectropion

Ectropian is the scientific term for exceedingly loose lower eyelids or "haw-eyedness." It is not a disabling condition like entropion but is unsightly and can create constant irritation because the drooping skin allows dust and dirt to collect in the eye socket.

Progressive Retinal Atrophy

Progressive retinal atrophy (PRA) is a hereditary eye disorder that can ultimately lead to blindness. There are two types—juvenile and adult.

The nerve layers at the back of the eye are particularly sensitive as they receive and process light stimuli. Any developmental change or damage to the eye of the unborn puppy may lead to atrophy of the light receptors. The disease can be detected in very young puppies with an ophthalmoscope.

Vaccine Sensitivity

Most Bernese Mountain Dog breeders have initiated the necessary inoculation series for their puppies by the time they are eight weeks of age. These inoculations protect the puppies against hepatitis, leptospirosis, distemper, and canine parvovirus.

It is extremely important that new owners follow the breeder's recommendations on inoculations. Some Berner puppies can be extremely sensitive to the 5, 6, and 7 in 1 modified live vaccines. Some get very ill within two or three days of receiving the vaccines or a couple of weeks later. In other cases, seizures and or symptoms of hypothyroidism, liver and kidney problems, or heart complications show up several years later to a greater or lesser degree.

It is critical that a veterinarian who is not experienced in treating Bernese Mountain Dogs be advised of any recommendations made by the breeder.

All dogs have their own unique personalities. Obtaining a Bernese Mountain Dog from a reputable breeder and proper care and treatment will help ensure sound health and temperament.

QUESTIONS AND ANSWERS

All breeds of dog have genetic problems that must be paid attention to, and just because a male or female does not evidence problems, it does not mean their pedigrees are free of something that might be entirely incapacitating. Again, rely upon recommendations from national kennel clubs or local breed clubs when looking for a breeder.

As we have mentioned previously, do not be surprised if a concerned breeder asks many questions about you and the environment in which your Berner will be raised. Good breeders are just as concerned with the quality of the homes to which their dogs are going as you, the buyer, are in obtaining a sound and healthy dog.

Do not think a good Berner puppy can only come from a large kennel. On the contrary, today many of the best breeders raise dogs in their homes as a hobby. It is important, however, that you not allow yourself to fall into the hands of an irresponsible "backyard breeder."

Backyard breeders separate themselves from hobby breeders in their total lack of regard for the health of their breeding stock. They do not test their stock for genetic problems, nor are they concerned with how or where their puppies are raised. A good question to ask a Berner breeder is: "What do you do with your dogs?" Dedicated breeders are involved in many activities with their dogs—showing, obedience, carting, agility—the list could conceivably go on and on. The backyard breeder does nothing more than breed and sell.

We offer one important bit of advice to the prospective Berner buyer. If the person is attempting to sell you a puppy with no questions asked—go elsewhere!

RECOGNIZING A HEALTHY PUPPY

Berner breeders never release their puppies until they have been given their first "puppy shots." Nursing puppies receive temporary immunization from their mother. Once weaned, however, a puppy is highly susceptible to many infectious diseases, which can be transmitted via the hands and clothing of people. Therefore, it behooves you to make sure your puppy is fully inoculated before he leaves his home environment and to know when any additional inoculations should be given.

A healthy puppy should be strong and sturdy to the touch and have a soft, lustrous coat.

Above all, the Berner puppy you buy should be happy, outgoing, and self-confident. The Berner's protective instinct develops in adulthood. A shy or suspicious puppy is definitely a poor choice, as is one that appears sick and listless. Selecting a puppy of that sort because you feel sorry for him will undoubtedly lead to heartache and difficulty, to say nothing of the veterinary costs that you may incur in getting the puppy well.

Ask the breeder if it is possible to take the puppy you are interested in away from his littermates into another room or another part of the kennel. The smells will remain the same for the puppy, so he should still feel secure and maintain his outgoing personality. This will give you an opportunity to inspect the puppy more closely.

A healthy little Berner puppy will be strong and sturdy to the touch—plump but never obese and bloated, nor, on the other hand, scrawny looking and undernourished. The inside of the puppy's ears should be pink and clean. Dark discharge or a bad odor could indicate ear mites, a sure sign of poor maintenance. The healthy Berner puppy's breath smells sweet—well, maybe not exactly sweet, but that unique smell dog breeders lovingly call "puppy breath." The teeth are clean and white, and there should never be any malformation of the mouth or jaw. The puppy's eyes should be clear, bright, and have a soft, almost wise look, so typical of a Berner baby. Eyes that appear runny and irritated indicate serious problems. There should be no sign of discharge from the nose, nor should it be crusted or runny. Coughing or diarrhea are danger signals, as are any eruptions on the skin. The coat should be soft and lustrous.

The healthy Berner puppy's front legs should be straight as posts, strong, and true. Rolly-polly Berner puppies will appear active, agile, and strong, although they may stumble over their own feet occasionally. Do not mistake this for unsoundness, but if you have any doubts, discuss them with the breeder.

Male or Female?

While both the male and the female are capable of becoming excellent companions, do consider the fact that a male Berner will be larger, sometimes 10 or even 15 pounds heavier than his sister, and he will have all the grandeur and muscle power to go with the extra weight. Give serious consideration to your own strength and stature.

Whether male or female, the Bernese Mountain Dog is capable of becoming a wonderful, lifelong companion. However, do consider that a male Berner will weigh 10 or 15 pounds heavier than a female.

Although good looks and a charismatic personality are part of a dog's success in the show ring, they are not everything. Consult the breed standard for an example of an ideal Bernese Mountain Dog.

I do find males to be more predictable and conscientious than the females, which tend to be more pushy and demanding. Males are truly wonderful with children and, more often than not, head off aggression with a smile. The male Bernese Mountain Dog is far less apt to lift his leg and mark inside of your home than some of the smaller breeds. They are also not as inclined to start a fight with other dogs.

Females have their semiannual heat cycles, which can commence as early as six or seven months of age. During these heat cycles of approximately 21 days, the female must be confined to avoid becoming impregnated. Do not allow your female to be out of doors alone even for a minute when she is in season. Clever neighborhood Lotharios will be waiting to pounce the instant your back is turned.

There is a bloody discharge that accompanies estrus, and your female must be kept where she will not soil her surroundings. Like everything else about the Bernese Mountain Dog, the bloody discharge is lots in comparison to smaller breeds where the discharge is usually referred to as "spotting." There are "britches" sold at pet shops that assist in keeping the female in heat from soiling the area in which she lives. She must also be carefully watched to prevent males from gaining access to her. Do not expect the "marauding male" to be deterred by the britches should your female have them on!

Both of these sexually related problems can be avoided by having the pet Berner altered. Spaying the female and neutering the male saves the pet owner all the headaches of sexually related problems without changing the character of your Berner. If there is any change at all in the altered Berner, it is in making the dog an even more amiable companion. Above all, altering your pet precludes the possibility of its adding to the serious pet overpopulation problems that exist worldwide.

I advise anyone interested in the breed not to begin their relationship with it by hunting for a "Berner to breed." Begin your life with the breed by finding that one special Berner that has your name on him. Read and learn all you can about the breed, and then, after you are absolutely sure that you simply cannot live without a Berner in your life—and only then— should you even begin to think about breeding.

Selecting a Show-Prospect Puppy

If you are considering a show career for your puppy, all the foregoing regarding soundness and health applies as well. It must be remembered, though, that spaying and castration are not reversible procedures and once done, eliminate the possibility of ever breeding or showing your Berner in conformation shows. Altered dogs can, however, be shown in obedience trials and many other competitive events.

There are a good number of additional points to be considered for the show dog as well. First, the most any breeder can offer is an opinion on the "show potential" of a particular puppy. The most promising eight-week-old Berner puppy can grow up to be an average adult. A breeder has no control over this. It is sometimes said that an unknowing new owner can ruin a "show prospect" in about three weeks with improper feeding and exercise, and this certainly holds true with a giant-breed puppy like the Berner.

Any predictions breeders make about a puppy's future are based upon their experience with past litters that have produced winning show dogs. It is obvious that the more successful a breeder has been in producing winning Berners over the years, the broader his or her base of comparison will be.

Although Berner puppies are adorable and often hard to resist, they may not be the best choice for some people. Carefully consider whether a puppy or adult Berner is right for your lifestyle.

Maintaining your Berner's original diet will help eliminate stomach problems and digestive upset. If you need to make adjustments, do so gradually.

A puppy's potential as a show dog is determined by how closely he adheres to the demands of the standard of the breed. While most breeders concur there is no such thing as "a sure thing" when it comes to predicting winners, they are also quick to agree the older a puppy is, the better your chances are of making any predictions.

It makes little difference to the owner of a pet if his Berner is a little high in the rear or if he doesn't have all the exact curves, angles, or markings the standard calls for. These faults do not interfere with a Berner becoming a healthy, loving companion. However, these flaws would keep that Berner from a top show career.

While it certainly behooves the prospective buyer of a show-prospect puppy to be as familiar with the standard of the breed as possible, it is even more important for the buyer to put himself or herself into the hands of a successful and respected breeder of winning Berners. The experienced breeder knows there are certain age-related shortcomings in a young Berner that maturity will take care of, and there are other faults that completely eliminate the puppy from consideration as a show prospect. Breeders are always looking for the right homes in which to place their show-prospect puppies. They can be particularly helpful when they know you plan to show one of their dogs.

The important thing to remember in choosing your first show prospect is that "cuteness" may not be consistent with quality. While showmanship and a charismatic personality are critical to a show dog's success in the ring, those qualities are the frosting on the cake, so to speak. They are the characteristics that put the well-made Berner over the top.

An extroverted or particularly loving puppy in the litter might decide he belongs to you. If you are simply looking for a pet, that is the puppy for you. However, if you are genuinely interested in showing your Berner, you must keep your head and, without disregarding good temperament, give serious consideration to what the standard says a show-type Bernese Mountain Dog must be.

The complete standard of the breed is presented in this book, and there are also a number of other books that can assist the newcomer in learning more about the breed and about showing dogs in general.

PUPPY OR ADULT?

A young puppy is not your only option when contemplating the purchase of a Berner. In some cases, an adult dog may be just the answer. It certainly eliminates the trials and tribulations of housetraining, chewing, and the myriad other problems associated with a young puppy.

If there are small children in the family, an adult Berner that is used to children would be an ideal choice. He will need far less attention and training, and child-wise adult Berners seem to take adoption on by second nature.

Sometimes adult Berners are available from homes or kennels breeding show dogs. Retired from the ring or no longer being used for breeding, the breeder realizes the older dog would be far happier in a family situation where he can watch TV, take hikes, and be a part of a family instead of living out his life in a kennel run.

Fully mature Berners can also be available through Berner clubs and organizations. These dogs, thoroughly evaluated by the respective organization, can prove to be wonderful companions once they are rehomed.

Adult Berners can adjust to their new homes with relative ease. Most new owners are amazed at how quickly it all happens and how quickly these adults become devoted to their new families! After all, a Berner lives to have his own person or family to love and protect, and even those raised in a kennel seem to "blossom" in a family environment.

An adult Berner that has been given kind and loving care in his previous home could be the perfect answer for the elderly or someone who is forced to be away from home during the day. While it would be unreasonable to expect a young puppy not to relieve himself in the house while you are gone for more than just a few hours, it would be surprising to find a housetrained Berner that would even consider relieving himself in the home in which he lives.

A few adult Berners may have become set in their ways, and while you may not have to contend with the problems of puppyhood, do realize there is the rare adult that might have developed habits that do not entirely suit you or your lifestyle. Arrange to bring an adult Berner into your home on a trial basis. That way neither you nor the dog will be obligated should either of you decide you are incompatible.

IMPORTANT PAPERS

The purchase of any purebred dog entitles you to some very important documents: a health record containing a worming schedule and an inoculation list, a copy of the dog's pedigree, the registration certificate, and last but far from least, a sales contract.

Health Record

Most Berner puppies have had their first vaccine by the time they are six to eight weeks of age. These vaccines must be continued every three to four weeks until three or four have been given. The inoculations temporarily protect the puppies against distemper, hepatitis, leptospirosis, and canine parvovirus. Depending on where the breeder is located, puppies may also be vaccinated against coronavirus and Lyme's disease. In most cases, rabies inoculations are not given until a puppy is four months of age or older.

There is a set series of inoculations developed to combat these infectious diseases, and it is extremely important that you obtain a record of exactly what type of shots your puppy has been given and the dates upon which the shots were administered. Discuss this important issue with the breeder so that the veterinarian you choose will be able to continue with the appropriate inoculation series as needed.

When you purchase your Berner, the breeder should supply you with the following important documents: a health record, a copy of the dog's pedigree, the registration certificate, and a sales contract.

Treating your Bernese Mountain Dog with love and respect and providing him with the proper socialization will enable him to become a well-adjusted adult dog.

Pedigree

The pedigree is your dog's "family tree." The breeder must supply you with a copy of this document authenticating your puppy's ancestry back to at least the third generation. All purebred dogs have a pedigree. The pedigree does not imply that a dog is of show quality. It is simply a chronological list of his ancestors.

Registration Certificate

The registration certificate is the canine world's "birth certificate." This certificate is issued by a country's governing kennel club. When you transfer the ownership of your Berner from the breeder's name to your own name, the transaction is entered on this certificate, and once mailed to the kennel club, it is permanently recorded in their computerized files. Keep all of these documents in a safe place, as you will need them when you visit your veterinarian for orthopedic evaluation films or if you ever wish to breed or show your Berner.

Diet Sheet

Your Berner is the happy, healthy puppy he is because the breeder has been carefully feeding and caring for him. Every breeder we know has his own particular way of doing this. Most breeders give the new owner a written record that details the amount and kind of food a puppy has been receiving. Follow these recommendations to the letter at least for the first month or two after the puppy comes to live with you.

The diet sheet should indicate the number of times a day your puppy has been accustomed to being fed and the kind of vitamin supplementation, if any, he has been receiving. Following the prescribed procedure will reduce the chance of upset stomach and loose stools.

That said, each puppy's nutritional requirements will be different— even from his siblings. Every dog in my home eats a different amount and type of food based upon his or her special needs. Pay attention to your dog's condition.

Usually, a breeder's diet sheet projects the increases and changes in food that will be necessary as your puppy grows from week to week. If the sheet does not include this information, ask the breeder for suggestions regarding increases and the eventual changeover to adult food.

In the unlikely event you are not supplied with a diet sheet by the breeder and are unable to get one, your veterinarian will be able to advise you in this respect. There are countless foods now being

Socialization is an essential part of your Berner's development. Taking him to basic obedience classes will help him accept unfamiliar dogs more readily.

manufactured expressly to meet the nutritional needs of puppies and growing dogs. A trip down the pet aisle at your supermarket or pet supply store will prove just how many choices you have. There are two important tips to remember: Read labels carefully for content, and when dealing with established, reliable manufacturers, you are more likely to get what you pay for.

Sales Contract

The reputable Bernese Mountain Dog breeder will supply a written agreement that lists everything that he or she is responsible for in connection with the sale of the dog described. The contract will also list all the things the buyer is responsible for before the sale is actually final. The contract should be dated and signed by both the seller and the buyer. Sales contracts vary, but all assurances and anything that is an exception to the outright and final sale should be itemized. Some of these conditions should be:

• Sale is contingent upon the dog passing a veterinarian's examination within 24–48 hours after he leaves the seller's premises and a clear statement of refund policy.

• The contract should include any conditions prevailing regarding the seller's requirement for neutering of dog sold.

• There should be an indication that a "limited registration" accompanies the dog (that is, the dog is ineligible to have offspring registered by the AKC).

• The contract should include arrangements that must be followed in the event the buyer is unable to keep the dog, regardless of length of time that elapses after sale.

• Any conditions that exist should be listed in the event that the dog develops genetic bone, eye, or any other relevant genetic disorders at maturity.

TEMPERAMENT AND SOCIALIZATION

Temperament is both inherited and learned. Inherited good temperament can be ruined by poor treatment and lack of proper socialization. A Berner puppy that has inherited bad temperament is a poor risk as a show dog and should certainly never be bred. In fact, a Bernese Mountain Dog with poor temperament is entirely untypical of the breed and is not suitable to be kept as a pet. Therefore, it is critical that you obtain a happy puppy from a breeder who is determined to produce good temperaments and has taken all the necessary steps to provide the early socialization necessary.

Temperaments in the same litter can range from strong-willed and outgoing on the high end of the scale to reserved and retiring at the low end. A puppy that is so bold and strong-willed as to be foolhardy and uncontrollable could easily be a difficult adult that needs a very firm hand. In a breed as strong as a Berner, this would hardly be a dog for the owner who is mild and reserved in demeanor or frail in physique.

How often and how much you feed your dog depends on his age and activity level. A dog that is active and energetic will require more food than one that has a less strenuous lifestyle.

55

In every human-canine relationship there must be a pack leader and a follower. In order to achieve his full potential, the Berner must have an owner who remains in charge at all times. The Berner himself wants and needs this kind of relationship.

It is important to remember that a Berner puppy may be as happy as a clam living at home with you and your family, but if the socialization started by the breeder is not continued, that sunny disposition will not extend outside your front door. From the day the young Berner arrives at your home, you must be committed to accompanying him upon an unending pilgrimage to meet and coexist with all human beings and animals.

Do not worry about the Berner's protective instinct. This comes with maturity. Never encourage aggressive behavior on the part of your puppy, nor should there be any reason for your puppy to fear strangers. If your puppy backs off from a stranger, give the person a treat to offer him. You must insist your young Berner be amenable to the attention of any strangers you approve of, regardless of sex, age, or race. It is not up to your puppy to decide who he will or will not tolerate. You are in charge. You must call the shots.

If your Berner has a show career in his future, there are other things in addition to just being handled that will have to be taught. All show dogs must learn to have their mouths opened and inspected by the judge. The judge must be able to check the teeth. Males must be accustomed to having their testicles touched, as the dog show judge must determine that all male dogs are "complete," which means there are two normal-sized testicles in the scrotum. These inspections must begin in puppyhood and done on a regular and continuing basis.

All Berners must learn to get along with other dogs as well as with humans. If you are fortunate enough to have a "puppy preschool" or dog training class nearby, attend with as much regularity as you possibly can. A young Berner that has been regularly exposed to other dogs from puppyhood will learn to adapt and accept them much more readily than one that seldom ever sees strange dogs.

THE ADOLESCENT BERNESE MOUNTAIN DOG

The Swiss say, "Three years a pup, three years an adult, and if you are lucky, three years an old dog."

The Bernese Mountain Dog is very slow to mature. Some lines develop a bit more quickly than others, but overall, Berners mature

Socializing your Bernese Mountain Dog with other animals and people at a young age will benefit him later in life.

more slowly than other breeds their size. At about six months, most Berner puppies become lanky and ungainly, growing in and out of proportion seemingly from one day to the next. Somewhere between 12 to 18 months, your Berner will have attained his full height. However, body and muscle development continue until three years of age in some lines and up to four or more in others.

The amount of food you give your Berner should be adjusted to how much he will readily consume at each meal. If the entire meal is eaten quickly, add a small amount to the next feeding and continue to do so as the need increases. This method will ensure that you give your puppy enough food, but you must also pay close attention to the dog's appearance and condition, as you never want a puppy to become overweight or obese.

At eight weeks of age, a Berner puppy is eating three to four meals a day. By the time he is three months old, the puppy can do well on two meals a day, with perhaps a snack in the middle of the day. If your puppy does not eat the food offered, he is either not hungry or not well. Your dog will eat when he is hungry. If you suspect the dog is not well, a trip to the veterinarian is in order.

At six months, the Berner is beginning to mature mentally. It is extremely important to continually introduce the youngster to new experiences. This is critical to the Berner's stability. Somewhere between 8 and 18 months of age, adolescents often go through an insecure stage, becoming shy and fearful. It is important not to become pushy and insistent at this time. It is a temporary stage—sometimes lasting only a week or two—but speaking to your breeder about their experiences in this situation can prove helpful.

At this point, Berners, especially male Berners, begin to test their ability to dominate. Someone has to make the rules. Your Berner is really asking if you are the rule maker or if he should do so on his own. You are the one who must provide the answer.

This adolescent period is a particularly important one as it is the time your Berner must learn all the household and social rules by which he will live for the rest of his life. The Berner's adolescent period can be as exasperating as a child's. Rest assured, with continued consistency and love, you will both survive the trying times. Your patience and commitment during this period will not only produce an obedient canine good citizen, but will forge a bond between the two of you that will grow and ripen into a wonderful relationship.

STANDARD for the Bernese Mountain Dog

As far back in time as the Bernese Mountain Dog can be traced, the same characteristics have been valued in the breed: intelligence, versatility, a calm nature, and the willingness to step into any role required. These characteristics typify the breed and remain paramount in the minds of breeders who champion the cause of the Bernese Mountain Dog today.

It should be noted that attempts to classify and name the important characteristics of a breed—both mental and physical—were the forerunners of what are known as "breed standards" today. The original standards were written by knowledgeable individuals in the breed for their peers. The descriptions were used primarily as checklists or blueprints to breed by, and they served as reminders so that important points of conformation would not be lost.

Today's Bernese Mountain Dog breed standard describes a dog that is entirely capable of performing the duties he has been called upon to perform for thousands of years. It includes a description of ideal structure, temperament, coat and color, and the manner in

The Bernese Mountain Dog is known for his handsome appearance and gentle manner.

The Bernese Mountain Dog's dark-brown eyes should convey an intelligent and animated expression.

which the breed moves. All of these descriptions relate directly to the breed's original purpose.

As stated, breed standards are used by breeders to assist them in breeding toward this goal of perfection. While no dog is absolutely perfect, the dogs that adhere closest to the ideal are what breeders will determine are show or breeding stock, and the dogs that deviate to any extent are considered companion or pet stock.

The standard is also used by dog show judges to compare actual dogs to the ideal. The dog adhering closest to this ideal is then the winner of his class and so on down the line.

AKC STANDARD FOR THE BERNESE MOUNTAIN DOG

General Appearance—The Bernese Mountain Dog is a striking, tri-colored, large dog. He is sturdy and balanced. He is intelligent, strong and agile enough to do the draft and droving work for which he was used in the mountainous regions of his origin. Dogs appear masculine, while bitches are distinctly feminine.

Size, Proportion, Substance—Measured at the withers, dogs are 25 to 27 ¹/₂ inches; bitches are 23 to 26 inches. Though appearing square, Bernese Mountain Dogs are slightly longer in

According to the standard, the ideal Bernese Mountain Dog is capable of performing the duties he has been called upon to perform for thousands for years.

Striking in appearance, the Bernese Mountain Dog is sturdy and well-balanced.

body than they are tall. Sturdy bone is of great importance. The body is full.

Head—*Expression* is intelligent, animated and gentle. The *eyes* are dark brown and slightly oval in shape with close-fitting eyelids. Inverted or everted eyelids are serious faults. Blue eye color is a disqualification. The *ears* are medium sized, set high, triangular in shape, gently rounded at the tip, and hang close to the head when in repose. When the Bernese Mountain Dog is alert, the ears are brought forward and raised at the base; the top of the ear is level with the top of the skull. The *skull* is flat on top and broad, with a slight furrow and a well-defined, but not exaggerated stop. The *muzzle* is strong and straight. The *nose* is always black. The *lips* are clean and, as the Bernese Mountain Dog is a dry-mouthed breed, the flews are only slightly developed. The *teeth* meet in a scissors bite. An overshot or undershot bite is a serious fault. Dentition is complete. **Neck, Topline, Body**—The *neck* is strong, muscular and of medium length. The *topline* is level from the withers to the croup. The chest is deep and capacious with well-sprung, but not barrel-shaped, ribs and brisket reaching at least to the elbows. The back is broad and

The Bernese Mountain Dog's tri-colored coat is thick, moderately long, and slightly wavy or straight.

The natural gait of the Berner is a slow trot; however, he is capable of speed and agility during draft and droving work.

firm. The *loin* is strong. The *croup* is broad and smoothly rounded to the tail insertion. The *tail* is bushy. It should be carried low when in repose. An upward swirl is permissible when the dog is alert, but the tail may never curl or be carried over the back. The bones in the tail should feel straight and should reach to the hock joint or below. A kink in the tail is a fault.

Forequarters—The shoulders are moderately laid back, flat-lying, well-muscled and never loose. The *legs* are straight and strong and the *elbows* are well under the shoulder when the dog is standing. The *pasterns* slope very slightly, but are never weak. *Dewclaws* may be removed. The feet are round and compact with well-arched toes.

Hindquarters—The *thighs* are broad, strong and muscular. The *stifles* are moderately bent and taper smoothly into the hocks. The *hocks* are well let down and straight as viewed from the rear. *Dewclaws* should be removed. *Feet* are compact and turn neither in nor out.

Coat—The *coat* is thick, moderately long and slightly wavy or straight. It has a bright natural sheen. Extremely curly or extremely dull-looking coats are undesirable. The Bernese Mountain Dog is shown in natural coat and undue trimming is to be discouraged.

Color and Markings—The Bernese Mountain Dog is tri-colored. The ground color is jet black. The markings are rich rust and clear white. Symmetry of markings is desired. Rust appears over each eye, on the cheeks reaching to at least the corner of the mouth, on each side of the chest, on all four legs, and under the tail. There is a white blaze and muzzle band. A white marking on the chest typically forms an inverted cross. The tip of the tail is white. White on the feet is desired but must not extend higher than the pasterns. Markings other than described are to be faulted in direct relationship to the extent of the deviation. White legs or a white collar are serious faults. Any ground color other than black is a disqualification.

Gait—The natural working gait of the Bernese Mountain Dog is a slow trot. However, in keeping with his use in draft and droving work, he is capable of speed and agility. There is good reach in front. Powerful drive from the rear is transmitted through a level back. There is no wasted action. Front and rear legs on each side follow through in the same plane. At increased speed, legs tend to converge toward the center line.

Temperament—The *temperament* is self-confident, alert and good-natured, never sharp or shy. The Bernese Mountain Dog should stand steady, though may remain aloof to the attentions of strangers.

DISQUALIFICATIONS
Blue eye color.
Any ground color other than black.
Approved February 10, 1990
Effective March 28, 1990

Because the Bernese Mountain Dog is not a high-energy breed, he does not require a diet that is high in fat or protein.

CARING for Your Bernese Mountain Dog

FEEDING AND NUTRITION

F ollowing the diet sheet provided by the breeder is the best way to make sure your Berner puppy is obtaining the right amount and the correct type of food for his age. Do your best not to change the puppy's diet and he will be far less apt to run into digestive problems and diarrhea. Diarrhea is something that is very serious in young puppies. Puppies with diarrhea can dehydrate very rapidly, causing severe problems and even death.

If it is necessary to change your puppy's diet for any reason, it should never be done abruptly. Begin by adding a quarter-cup of the new food and reduce the old product by the same amount. Gradually increase the amount of the new food over a week or ten days until the meal consists entirely of the new product. A puppy's digestive system is extremely delicate. Any changes you make in what he eats should be done carefully and slowly.

The amount of food you give your Berner puppy should also be adjusted carefully. Give the puppy all he will eat within five minutes (certainly no longer than ten) from the time you put the food dish down. Take the dish up after that amount of time has elapsed. If the puppy consumes the entire meal, add a small amount to the next meal, balancing what you add with what the puppy will eat.

There is the occasional Berner puppy that is a true glutton, and he will eat more than he needs to stay healthy. A good rule of thumb—you should be able to feel the ribs and

Proper nutrition is imperative to your Berner's good health. Provide him with a balanced and nutritious diet and carefully monitor his weight.

Puppies will try to eat everything. Feeding your Berner a quality brand of dog food will help him grow into a strong, sound adult dog.

backbone with just a slight layer of fat and muscle over them. The puppy should be firm to the touch and not sloppy with rolls of loose flesh.

Because the Bernese is a slow-maturing breed, the diet you feed must accommodate that kind of development. The food you give is not intended to promote growth or facilitate high performance. It is especially important to avoid excessive weight gain during the puppy's first year, as excess weight exacts a heavy toll on the slowly developing skeletal structure of a Bernese Mountain Dog. The Berner's framework is extremely vulnerable during this early period of life, and you must do your utmost to avoid any undue stress being placed on it.

Considering what we now know about bloat and torsion, avoiding large meals is recommended. Better to feed smaller meals two or even three times daily, instead of one large meal.

Balanced Diets

In the US, dog foods must meet standards set by the Subcommittee on Canine Nutrition of the National Research Council in order to qualify as "complete and balanced." As proof of compliance, dog food manufacturers list the ingredients of their product on every box, bag, or can. The ingredients are listed by weight in descending order.

A Bernese Mountain Dog does not need a high-fat or high-protein diet because this is not a high-energy breed. We recommend keeping the protein content of a Berner's diet down to a level of 22 to 26 percent. Fat content should not exceed much above a total of 14 to 18 percent. Fat is the last thing you want your Berner to be!

Do not feed your Berner sugar products, and avoid products that contain sugar to any high degree. Excessive amounts of these sugars can lead to severe dental problems and unwanted weight gain.

To achieve optimum health and condition, make sure your Berner has a constant supply of fresh, clean water and a balanced diet containing the essential nutrients in correct proportions. This can be achieved with a good quality kibble to which a small amount of canned, fresh, or cooked meat can be added. Pet stores and supermarkets all carry a wide selection of foods manufactured by respected firms. I am inclined to believe that using only one brand of commercial dog food for a dog's entire life creates allergies and an intolerance to certain other food types. I feed a balanced, high-

A nutritious diet and proper exercise will keep your Bernese Mountain Dog in excellent physical condition.

quality kibble but offer some variety in the protein additive.

I do not recommend continually switching from one brand to the next, but I do make gradual and occasional changes. An important thing to remember in selecting from these foods is that all dogs are meat-eating animals. Animal protein and fats are absolutely essential—in the right balance—to the well-being of all breeds of dog.

Supplementation

A great deal of controversy exists today regarding the orthopedic problems that exist in all dogs, such as hip, elbow, and patella (knee)

Water is an essential part of your Bernese Mountain Dog's diet. Provide him with a constant supply of clean, fresh water.

dysplasia. Long-standing popular opinion has always dictated that these problems, and a wide variety of chronic skin conditions, are entirely hereditary. However, there is growing contingency that overuse of mineral and vitamin supplements in puppies and young dogs can exacerbate, if not cause, these ailments.

When vitamins are used for convalescence or injury, the prescribed amount should never be exceeded. Some breeders insist all recommended dosages be cut in half when used with the heavily fortified commercial foods of the day. The only supplements I believe in are Vitamin C and perhaps some of the glucosoamine and choondrotin products now on the market that promote healthy joints and flexibility.

Dogs do not care if food looks like a hot dog or a wedge of cheese. They only care about the food's smell and its taste. Products manufactured to look like other foods are designed to appeal to the humans who buy them. These foods often contain high amounts of preservatives, sugars, and dyes—none of which are suitable for your dog.

Special Diets

There are now any number of commercially prepared diets for dogs with special dietary needs. The overweight, underweight, or geriatric dog can have his nutritional needs met, as can puppies and growing dogs. The calorie content of these foods is adjusted accordingly.

Common sense must prevail. What works for humans works for dogs as well—too many calories and too little exercise will increase weight; stepping up exercise and reducing the calorie count will bring weight down.

GROOMING AND BATHING

Berners do not require any fancy clipping or trimming, and the correct coat is relatively easy to maintain. Grooming will not require much of your time or lots of equipment, but that is not to say that the breed needs no care at all in this respect. Regular brushing keeps the coat clean, odor-free, and healthy, to say nothing of the amount of hair you will not have to vacuum up off the floor and sofa.

You will need to invest in a good short-toothed undercoat rake, a "slicker" brush, which has short-angled bristles, a steel comb, and a nail clipper. A comb that has teeth divided between fine and coarse is ideal. Consider the fact you will be using this equipment for many years, so buy the best of these items that you can afford.

Regularly brushing your Berner's coat will keep it clean, odor-free, and healthy.

Puppies have a soft, fluffy coat that seems to attract dirt. It begins to change into an adult coat at around four to five months, but the change is not complete until the dog is somewhere between one and one-and-a-half years old. If a Berner has been spayed or neutered, the coats can sometimes grow longer and/or thicker with more undercoat. This type of coat may require more brushing and care.

Shaving the coat of a Berner does not make the dog cooler in hot weather. In fact, it is a dangerous thing to do because the dog becomes susceptible to sunburn and heat stroke. The double coat of the Bernese Mountain Dog not only keeps the breed warm in cold weather, but also insulates and cools in the heat. Berners normally shed most of their undercoats when it is hot around the beginning summer, and this is enough to keep them cool.

Regular grooming gives you the opportunity to stay on top of your dog's home health care needs. Such things as trimming nails, cleaning ears, and checking teeth can be attended to at this time as well.

The Berner has a double coat—a soft undercoat and a coarser outer coat. This type of coat sheds out and does not pack in and mat as much as the coat of a Samoyed or a Chow Chow. You can brush a Berner daily if you want (they do enjoy it!), but brushing should take place at least weekly.

Part the hair and brush the coat from the skin out to prevent mats. When the coat is shedding, you will want to brush daily if you possibly can. This helps get out all of the dead coat, making it easier for the new coat to come in. During this time mats are inclined to occur behind the ears, under the "arms," and in the "pants" of the rear legs.

Nails

Puppyhood is a good time to accustom your Berner to having his nails trimmed and feet inspected. Always inspect your dog's feet for cracked pads. Check between the toes for splinters and thorns, paying particular attention to any swollen or tender areas. This is also a good time to pick up each foot and carefully clip the hair that grows between the pads. Cut the hair flush with the bottom of the foot.

We suggest attending to your dog's nails at least every other week. Long nails on a Berner are not only unattractive, they spread and

Parasites can harm your dog. When your dog is through playing outside, check his coat thoroughly for any insect or parasite that may cause infection.

The Berner's double coat keeps him warm in cold weather and insulates and cools him in the heat.

Untrimmed nails can spread and weaken your dog's feet. Trimming them every other week will keep them attractive and healthy.

weaken the foot. The nails of a Berner that isn't exercising outdoors on rough terrain will grow long very quickly. Do not allow the nails to become overgrown and then expect to cut them back easily. Each nail has a blood vessel running through the center called the quick. The quick grows close to the end of the nail and contains very sensitive nerve endings. If the nail is allowed to grow too long, it will be impossible to cut it back to a proper length without cutting into the quick. This causes severe pain to the dog and can also result in a great deal of bleeding that can be very difficult to stop.

Nails can be trimmed with canine nail clippers or an electric nail grinder (also called a drummel). If you prefer the drummel, use the fine grinding disc because this allows you to trim back the nail a little bit at a time, preventing any bleeding from occuring. Dark nails make it practically impossible to see where the quick ends, so regardless of which nail trimming device is used, you must proceed with caution and remove only a small portion of the nail at a time.

If the quick is nipped in the trimming process, there are any number of blood-clotting products available at pet shops that will almost immediately stem the flow of blood. It is wise to have one of these products on hand in case your dog breaks a nail in some way.

Ears

Berners tend to get ear infections easily. Keep the ears clean and odor-free. You can damage the inside of the ear when you probe too far, so I use a cotton ball on my fingertip moistened with warm soapy water. If you notice an offensive smell from the ear, take your dog to your vet at once.

Bathing

Regular brushing practically eliminates the need for giving your Berner a wet bath. However, a well-timed bath at the start of each period of heavy shedding can help to hasten the process and get that dead hair off and away. If you do have to bathe your dog, do not bathe him too often. Rinsing all shampoo residue out of the coat is extremely important. Soap that is allowed to remain on the coat or too many baths can rob the skin of its lubricating oils, and all kinds of skin problems can occur.

Bathing, rinsing, and drying the coat thoroughly and properly are chores that will take considerable time. Many Berner owners have this done professionally at a grooming shop. There are also self-service bath shops that are popping up all over the country that you can use. These shops have industrial-level grooming equipment that allow you to complete the project much more quickly and yet do it properly. In addition, once you've finished you can walk out the door and leave the mess behind.

No bath is complete without totally drying the coat. Always blow dry your Berner, continually brushing while the dryer is blowing on the coat. Never "cage dry," that is, having your dog sit in a cage while the hair dryer blows on him. This mats down the hair and leaves the undercoat damp.

Care should always be given to the state of your dog's teeth. If your dog has been accustomed to chewing hard dog biscuits or gnawing on large rawhide bones since puppyhood, it is unlikely that you will have any dental problems. This chewing activity assists in removing dental plaque, which is the major cause of tooth decay. Any sign of redness of the gums or tooth decay merits expert attention. Dogs with wet (drooling) mouths need more dental care than do dogs with drier mouths.

Grooming your Berner is a good way to keep on top of his physical condition. Gently running your hands along his body will help detect any lumps, bumps, or bruises that could be an indication of internal complications.

EXERCISE

The Berner that is given opportunity to exercise on his own, or even better, with you, is a much happier and healthier dog. Any dog that expends his energy in physical activity is far less apt to become mischievous and destructive in the home.

Needless to say, puppies and young dogs should never be forced to exercise. Young Bernese Mountain Dogs need the opportunity to exercise at will, but they also enjoy a long steady walk on lead or a romp through the park or on the local beach. However, until the dog is mature, and only if you have properly conditioned him like a young

Exercise provides your Bernese Mountain Dog with the opportunity to release excess energy or stress and stay in shape.

Bernese Mountain Dogs enjoy the outdoors and will gladly participate in a leisurely hike or walk.

human athlete would be, can he be exposed to any arduous or lengthy exercise. In Switzerland, only Berners that are at least three to six years old are used for hauling. Also, consider where you walk—soft ground is much better than pavement for your Berner's joints. Jogging on a paved path and too much stair climbing can be very hard on the developing bones and joints of the young Berner.

SOCIALIZATION

A young Berner that has never been exposed to strangers, traffic noises, or boisterous children could become confused and frightened. It is important that a Berner owner give his or her dog the opportunity to experience all of these situations gradually and with his trusted owner present for support.

Berner puppies are usually friendly and more than happy to accept strangers, but lack of maturity often makes them more reserved. A Berner that never meets an unusual situation or a stranger is understandably going to be somewhat upset at abrupt changes. It is absolutely imperative that you continue the socialization process while maintaining the pack leader role with your Berner as he matures.

A well-trained Berner can give you a feeling of security and still be a pleasant canine citizen. A properly-trained Berner knows he obeys your commands under all circumstances and that "No!" means just that—once you give that command he must stop whatever he is doing.

With the correct training and socialization, the Bernese Mountain Dog can succeed at any activity.

SPORT of Purebred Dogs

Welcome to the exciting and sometimes frustrating sport of dogs. No doubt you are trying to learn more about dogs or you wouldn't be deep into this book. This section covers the basics that may entice you, further your knowledge, and help you to understand the dog world.

Dog showing has been a very popular sport for a long time and has been taken quite seriously by some. Others only enjoy it as a hobby.

The Kennel Club in England was formed in 1859, the American Kennel Club was established in 1884, and the Canadian Kennel Club was formed in 1888. The purpose of these clubs was to register purebred dogs and maintain their stud books. In the beginning, the concept of registering dogs was not readily accepted. More than 36 million dogs have been enrolled in the AKC Stud Book since its inception in 1888. Presently, the kennel clubs not only register dogs, but adopt and enforce rules and regulations governing dog shows, obedience trials, and field trials. Over the years they have fostered and encouraged interest in the health and welfare of the purebred dog. They routinely donate funds to veterinary research for study on genetic disorders.

Below are the addresses of the kennel clubs in the United States, Great Britain, and Canada.

American Kennel Club
260 Madison Avenue
New York, NY 10016
or 5580 Centerview Drive,
Raleigh, NC 27606

The Kennel Club
1 Clarges Street
Picadilly, London, WIJ 8AB, England

The Canadian Kennel Club
89 Skyway Avenue
Suite 100
Etobicoke, Ontario, Canada M9W 6R4

Training your Bernese Mountain Dog for competition builds his confidence and strengthens the bond between you.

Today there are numerous activities that are enjoyable for both the dog and the handler. Some of the activities include conformation showing, obedience competition, tracking, agility, the Canine Good Citizen® Certificate, and a wide range of instinct tests that vary from breed to breed. Where you start depends upon your goals, which early on may not be readily apparent.

PUPPY KINDERGARTEN

Every puppy will benefit from this class. PKT is the foundation for all future dog activities from conformation to "couch potatoes." Pet owners should make an effort to attend, even if they never expect to show their dogs. The class is designed for puppies about three months of age with graduation at approximately five months of age. All the puppies will be in the same age group, and, even though some may be a little unruly, there should not be any real problem. This class will teach the puppy some beginning obedience. As in all obedience classes, the owner learns how to train his own dog. The PKT class gives the puppy the opportunity to interact with other puppies in the same age group and exposes him to strangers, which is very important. Some dogs grow up with behavior problems, one of them being fear of strangers. As you can see, there can be much to gain from this class.

There are some basic obedience exercises that every dog should learn. Some of these can be started with puppy kindergarten.

Sit

One way of teaching the sit is to have your dog on your left side, with the leash in your right hand, close to the collar. Pull up on the leash, and at the same time reach around his hindlegs with your left hand and tuck them in. As you are doing this say, "Rover, sit." Always use the dog's name when you give an active command. Some owners like to use a treat, holding it over the dog's head. The dog will need to sit to get the treat. Encourage the dog to hold the sit for a few seconds, which will eventually be the beginning of the sit/stay. Depending on how cooperative he is, you can rub him under the chin or stroke his back. It is a good time to establish eye contact.

Down

Sit the dog on your left side, and kneel down beside him with the leash in your right hand. Reach over him with your left hand and grasp his left foreleg. With your right hand, take his right foreleg and pull his legs forward while you say, "Beau, down." If he tries to get up, lean on his shoulder to encourage him to stay down. It will relax your dog if you stroke his back while he is down. Try to encourage him to stay down for a few seconds as preparation for the down/stay.

Having an energized and motivated attitude is conducive to successful dog training. It also helps to conduct the lessons in an area free of distractions and to keep them short, fun, and interesting.

Heel

The definition of heeling is the dog walking under control at your left heel. Your puppy will learn controlled walking in the puppy kindergarten class, which will eventually lead to heeling. Give the command "Rover, heel," and start off briskly with your left foot. Your leash is in your right hand, and your left hand is holding it about half way down. Your left hand should be able to control the leash, and there should be a little slack in it. You want him to walk with you with your leg somewhere between his nose and his shoulder. You need to encourage him to stay with you, not forging ahead or lagging behind you. It is best to keep him on a fairly short lead. Do not allow the lead to become tight. It is far better to give him a little jerk when necessary and remind him to heel. When you come to a halt, be prepared to physically make him sit. It takes practice to become coordinated. There are excellent books on training that you may wish to purchase. Your instructor should be able to recommend one for you.

The down command can be difficult for some dogs to master because it puts them in a submissive position.

Training your Bernese Mountain Dog to walk alongside of you while on a leash will enable the both of you to enjoy leisurely walks together.

Recall

Recall quite possibly is the most important exercise you will ever teach. It should be a pleasant experience. The puppy may learn to do random recalls while being attached to a long line such as a clothes line. Later, the exercise will start with the dog sitting and staying until called. The command is "Rover, come." Let your command be happy. You want your dog to come willingly and faithfully. The recall could save his life if he sneaks out the door. In practicing the recall, let him jump on you or touch you before you reach for him. If he is shy, then kneel down to his level. Reaching for the insecure dog could frighten him, and he may not be willing to come again in the future. Lots of praise and a treat would be in order whenever you do a recall. Under no circumstances should you ever correct your dog when he has come to you. Later, in formal obedience, your dog will be required to sit in front of you after recalling and then go to heel position.

CONFORMATION

Conformation showing is the oldest dog show sport. This type of showing is based on the dog's appearance—that is, his structure, movement, and attitude. When considering this type of showing, you need to be aware of your breed's standard and be able to evaluate your dog compared to that standard. The breeder of your puppy or other experienced breeders would be good sources for such an evaluation. Puppies can go through lots of changes over a period of time. Many puppies start out as promising hopefuls and then after maturing may be disappointing as show candidates. Even so, this should not deter them from being excellent pets.

Conformation training classes are usually offered by the local kennel or obedience clubs. These are excellent places for training puppies. The puppy should be able to walk on a lead before entering such a class. Proper ring procedure and technique for posing (stacking) the dog will be demonstrated, as well as gaiting the dog. Generally, certain patterns are used in the ring, such as the triangle or the "L." Conformation class, like the PKT class, will give your youngster the opportunity to socialize with different breeds of dog and humans, too.

It takes some time to learn the routine of conformation showing. Usually, one starts at the puppy matches that may be AKC sanctioned or fun matches. These matches are generally for puppies from 2 or 3 months to a year old, and there may be classes for the adult over the age of 12 months. Similar to point shows, the classes are divided by sex, and after completion of the classes in that breed or variety, the class winners compete for Best of Breed or Variety. The winner goes on to compete in the Group, and the Group winners compete for Best in Match. No championship points are awarded for match wins.

A few matches can be great training for puppies, even if there is no intention to go on showing. Matches enable the puppy to meet new people and be handled by a stranger—the judge. It also offers a change of environment, which broadens the horizon for both dog and handler. Matches and other dog activities boost the confidence of the handler, and especially the younger handlers.

Earning an AKC championship is built on a point system, which is different from Great Britain. To become an AKC Champion of Record, the dog must earn 15 points. The number of points earned each time depends upon the number of dogs in competition. The number of points available at each show depends upon the breed, its sex, and the location of the show. The United States is divided into ten AKC zones. Each zone has its own set of points. The purpose of

In conformation, your Bernese Mountain Dog will be judged on his overall appearance, including structure, movement, and attitude.

the zones is to try to equalize the points available from breed to breed and area to area. The AKC adjusts the point scale annually.

The number of points that can be won at a show are between one and five. Three-, four- and five-point wins are considered majors. Not only does the dog need 15 points won under 3 different judges, but those points must include 2 majors under 2 different judges. Canada also works on a point system, but majors are not required.

Males always show before bitches. The classes available to those seeking points are: Puppy (which may be divided into 6 to 9 months and 9 to 12 months); 12 to 18 months; Novice; Bred-by-Exhibitor; American-bred; and Open. The class winners of the same sex of each breed or variety compete against each other for Winners Dog and Winners Bitch. A Reserve Winners Dog and Reserve Winners Bitch are also awarded but do not carry any points unless the Winners win is disallowed by AKC. The Winners Dog and Bitch compete with the Specials (those dogs that have attained championship) for Best of Breed or Variety, Best of Winners, and Best of Opposite Sex. It is possible to pick up an extra point or even a major if the points are higher for the defeated winner than those of Best of Winners. The latter would get the higher total from the defeated winner.

Showing requires dedication and preparation, but most of all it should be enjoyable for both the dog and handler.

At an all-breed show, each Best of Breed or Variety winner will go on to his respective Group and then the Group winners will compete against each other for Best in Show. There are seven Groups: Sporting, Hounds, Working, Terriers, Toys, Non-Sporting, and Herding. Obviously, there are no Groups at speciality shows (those shows that have only one breed or a show such as the American Spaniel Club's Flushing Spaniel Show, which is for all flushing spaniel breeds).

Earning a championship in England is somewhat different since they do not have a point system. Challenge Certificates are awarded if the judge feels the dog is deserving, regardless of the number of dogs in competition. A dog must earn 3 Challenge Certificates under 3 different judges, with at least 1 of these Certificates being won after the age of 12 months. Competition is very strong and entries may be higher than they are in the US. The Kennel Club's Challenge Certificates are only available at championship shows.

In England, The Kennel Club regulations require that certain dogs, Border Collies and gundog breeds, qualify in a working capacity (i.e., obedience or field trials) before becoming a full champion. If they do not qualify in the working aspect, then they are designated a show champion, which is equivalent to the AKC's Champion of Record. A gundog may be granted the title of Field Trial Champion (FTCh.) if he passes all the tests in the field, but would also have to qualify in conformation before becoming a full champion. A Border Collie that earns the title of Obedience Champion (ObCh.) must also qualify in the conformation ring before becoming a champion.

The US doesn't have a designation full Champion, but does award for Dual and Triple Champions. The Dual Champion must be a Champion of Record, and either Champion Tracker, Herding Champion, Obedience Trial Champion, or Field Champion. Any dog that has been awarded the titles of Champion of Record, and any two of the following: Champion Tracker, Herding Champion, Obedience Trial Champion or Field Champion, may be designated as a Triple Champion.

The shows in England seem to put more emphasis on breeder judges than those in the US. There is much competition within the breeds. Therefore, the quality of the individual breeds should be very good. In the US we tend to have more "all around judges," (those that judge multiple breeds) and use the breeder judges at the specialty shows. Breeder judges are more familiar with their own breed as they are actively breeding that breed or did so at one time. Americans emphasize Group and Best in Show wins and promote them accordingly.

The shows in England can be very large and extend over several days, with the Groups being scheduled on different days. Though multi-day shows are not common in the US, there are cluster shows in which several different clubs will use the same show site over consecutive days.

Westminster Kennel Club is our most prestigious show, although the entry is limited to 2,500. In recent years, entry has been limited to champions. This show is more formal than the majority of the shows, with the judges wearing formal attire and the handlers fashionably dressed. In most instances, the quality of the dogs is superb. After all, it is a show of champions. It is a good show to study the AKC registered breeds and is by far the most exciting— especially since it is televised! WKC is one of the few shows in this country that is still benched. This means the dog must be in his benched area during the show hours, except when he is being groomed, is in the ring, or is being exercised.

Typically, the handlers are very particular about their appearances. They are careful not to wear something that will detract from their dogs, but will perhaps enhance them. American ring procedure is quite formal compared to that of other countries. There is a certain etiquette expected between the judge and exhibitor and among the other exhibitors. Of course, it is not always the case, but the judge is supposed to be polite, not engaging in small talk or acknowledging how well he knows the handler. There is a more informal and relaxed atmosphere at the shows in other countries. For instance, the dress code is more casual. I can see where this might be more fun for the exhibitor and especially for the novice. The US is very handler-oriented in many of the breeds. It is true, in most instances, that the experienced professional handler can better present the dog and will have a feel for what a judge likes.

In England, Crufts is The Kennel Club's own show and is most assuredly the largest dog show in the world. It's been known to have an entry of nearly 20,000, and the show lasts four days. Entry is only

Pictured here is "Alex" taking Best of Winners at the Cook Inlet Kennel Club.

gained by qualifying through winning in specified classes at another championship show. Westminster is strictly conformation, but Crufts exhibitors and spectators enjoy not only conformation, but obedience, agility, and a multitude of exhibitions, as well. Obedience was admitted in 1957 and agility in 1983.

If you are handling your own dog, please give some consideration to your apparel. The dress code at matches is more informal than at the point shows. However, you should wear something a little more appropriate than beach attire or ragged jeans and bare feet. If you check out the handlers and see what is presently fashionable, you'll catch on. Men usually dress with a shirt and tie and a nice sports coat. Whether you are male or female, you will want to wear comfortable clothes and shoes. You need to be able to run with your dog, and you certainly don't want to take a chance of falling and hurting yourself. Heaven forbid, if nothing else, you'll upset your dog. Women usually wear a dress or two-piece outfit, preferably with pockets to carry bait, brush, etc. In this case, men are the lucky ones with all their pockets. Ladies, think about where your dress will be if you

Handlers should wear comfortable clothing that complements their dogs and allows them to move about freely.

need to kneel on the floor, and also think about running. Does it allow freedom to do so?

You need to take along dog; crate; ex pen (if you use one); extra bedding; water pail and water; all required grooming equipment; table; chair for you; bait for dog and lunch for you and friends; and, last but not least, clean up materials, such as plastic bags, paper towels, and perhaps a damp towel—just in case. Don't forget your entry confirmation and directions to the show.

If you are showing in obedience, you may want to wear pants. Many of our top obedience handlers wear pants that are color-coordinated with their dogs. The philosophy is that imperfections in the black dog will be less obvious next to your black pants.

Whether you are showing in conformation, Junior Showmanship, or obedience, you need to watch the clock and be sure you are not late. It is customary to pick up your conformation armband a few minutes before the start of the class. They will not wait for you, and if you are on the show grounds and not in the ring, you will upset everyone. It's a little more complicated picking up your obedience armband if you show later in the class. If you have not picked it up and they get to your number, you may not be allowed to show. It's best to pick up your armband early, but be aware that you may show earlier than expected if other handlers don't pick up. Customarily, all conflicts should be discussed with the judge prior to the start of the class.

Junior Showmanship

The Junior Showmanship Class is a wonderful way to build self confidence, even if there are no aspirations of staying with the dog-show game later in life. Frequently, Junior Showmanship becomes the background of those who become successful exhibitors/handlers in the future. In some instances, it is taken very seriously, and success is measured in terms of wins. The Junior Handler is judged solely on his ability and skill in presenting his dog. The dog's conformation is not to be considered by the judge. Even so, the condition and grooming of the dog may be a reflection upon the handler.

Usually, the matches and point shows include different classes. The Junior Handler's dog may be entered in a breed or obedience class and even shown by another person in that class. Junior

Showmanship classes are usually divided by age and perhaps sex. The age is determined by the handler's age on the day of the show. The classes are:

Novice Junior for those at least 10 and under 14 years of age, who at the time of entry closing have not won 3 first places in a Novice Class at a licensed or member show.

Novice Senior for those at least 14 and under 18 years of age, who at the time of entry closing have not won 3 first places in a Novice Class at a licensed or member show.

Open Junior for those at least 10 and under 14 years of age, who at the time of entry closing have won at least 3 first places in a Novice Junior Showmanship Class at a licensed or member show with competition present.

Open Senior for those at least 14 and under 18 years of age, who at the time of entry closing have won at least 3 first places in a Novice Junior Showmanship Class at a licensed or member show with competition present.

Junior Handlers must include their AKC Junior Handler number on each show entry. This needs to be obtained from the AKC.

To become a Canine Good Citizen, your Berner must be able to perform a number of different behaviors, such as sitting politely for petting and accepting a friendly stranger.

Canine Good Citizen®

The AKC sponsors a program to encourage dog owners to train their dogs. Local clubs perform the pass/fail tests, and dogs that pass are awarded a Canine Good Citizen® Certificate. Proof of vaccination is required at the time of participation. The test includes:

1. Accepting a friendly stranger.
2. Sitting politely for petting.
3. Appearance and grooming.
4. Walking on a loose leash.
5. Walking through a crowd.
6. Sit and down on command/staying in place.
7. Come when called.
8. Reaction to another dog.
9. Reactions to distractions.
10. Supervised separation.

If more effort was made by pet owners to accomplish these exercises, fewer dogs would be cast off to the humane shelter.

Obedience

Obedience is necessary, without a doubt, but it can also become a wonderful hobby or even an obsession. Obedience classes and competition can provide wonderful companionship, not only with your dog but with your classmates or fellow competitors. It is always gratifying to discuss your dog's problems with others who have had similar experiences. The AKC acknowledged obedience around 1936, and it has changed tremendously even though many of the exercises are basically the same. Today, obedience competition is just that—very competitive. Even so, it is possible for every obedience exhibitor to come home a winner (by earning qualifying scores), even though he/she may not earn a placement in the class.

Most of the obedience titles are awarded after earning three qualifying scores (legs) in the appropriate class under three different judges. These classes offer a perfect score of 200, which is extremely rare. Each of the class exercises has its own point value. A leg is earned after receiving a score of at least 170 and at least 50 percent of the points available in each exercise. The titles are:

Companion Dog—CD

This is called the Novice Class and the exercises are:

1. Heel on leash and figure 8   40 points

2. Stand for examination	30 points
3. Heel free	40 points
4. Recall	30 points
5. Long sit—one minute	30 points
6. Long down—three minutes	30 points
Maximum total score	200 points

Companion Dog Excellent—CDX

This is the Open Class and the exercises are:

1. Heel off leash and figure 8	40 points
2. Drop on recall	30 points
3. Retrieve on flat	20 points
4. Retrieve over high jump	30 points
5. Broad jump	20 points
6. Long sit—three minutes (out of sight)	30 points
7. Long down—five minutes (out of sight)	30 points
Maximum total score	200 points

Utility Dog—UD

The Utility Class exercises are:

1. Signal exercise	40 points
2. Scent discrimination-Article 1	30 points
3. Scent discrimination-Article 2	30 points
4. Directed retrieve	30 points
5. Moving stand and examination	30 points
6. Directed jumping	40 points
Maximum total score	200 points

After achieving the UD title, you may feel inclined to go after the UDX and/or OTCh. The UDX (Utility Dog Excellent) title went into effect in January 1994. It is not easily attained. The title requires qualifying simultaneously ten times in Open B and Utility B, but not necessarily at consecutive shows.

The OTCh. (Obedience Trial Champion) is awarded after the dog has earned his UD and then goes on to earn 100 championship points, a first place in Utility, a first place in Open, and another first place in either class. The placements must be won under three different judges at all-breed obedience trials. The points are determined by the number of dogs competing in the Open B and Utility B classes. The OTCh. title precedes the dog's name.

Even if you don't plan to show your Berner, he will benefit from basic training by becoming a valued dog companion and member of the community.

Obedience matches (AKC-sanctioned, fun, and show and go) are often available. Usually, they are sponsored by the local obedience clubs. When preparing an obedience dog for a title, you will find matches very helpful. Fun matches and show and go matches are more lenient in allowing you to make corrections in the ring. This type of training is usually very necessary for the Open and Utility classes. AKC-sanctioned obedience matches do not allow corrections in the ring since they must abide by the AKC obedience regulations booklet. If you are interested in showing in obedience, you should contact the AKC for a copy of *Obedience Regulations.*

TRACKING

Tracking is officially classified as obedience. There are three tracking titles available: Tracking Dog (TD), Tracking Dog Excellent (TDX), and Variable Surface Tracking (VST). If all three tracking titles are obtained, then the dog officially becomes a CT (Champion Tracker). The CT will go in front of the dog's name.

A TD may be earned anytime and does not have to follow the other obedience titles. There are many exhibitors that prefer tracking to obedience, and there are others who do both.

Tracking Dog—TD

A dog must be certified by an AKC tracking judge that he is ready to perform in an AKC test. The AKC can provide the names of tracking judges in your area that you can contact for certification. Depending on where you live, you may have to travel a distance if there is no local tracking judge nearby. The certification track will be equivalent to a regular AKC track. A regulation track must be 440 to 500 yards long, with at least two right-angle turns out in the open. The track will be aged 30 minutes to 2 hours. The handler has two starting flags at the beginning of the track to indicate the direction started. The dog works on a harness and 40-foot lead and must work at least 20 feet in front of the handler. An article (either a dark glove or wallet) will be dropped at the end of the track, and the dog must indicate it but not necessarily retrieve it.

People always ask what the dog tracks. Initially, the beginner on the short-aged track tracks the tracklayer. Eventually, the dog learns to track the disturbed vegetation and learns to differentiate between tracks. Getting started with tracking requires reading the AKC regulations and a good book on tracking, plus finding other tracking

This Bernese Mountain Dog effortlessly flies over the bar jump.

enthusiasts. Work on the buddy system. That is, lay tracks for each other so you can practice blind tracks. It is possible to train on your own, but if you are a beginner, it is a lot more entertaining to track with a buddy. It's rewarding seeing the dog use his natural ability.

Tracking Dog Excellent—TDX

The TDX track is 800 to 1000 yards long and is aged 3 to 5 hours. There will be five to seven turns. An article is left at the starting flag, and three other articles must be indicated on the track. There is only one flag at the start, so it is a blind start. Approximately one and a half hours after the track is laid, two tracklayers will cross over the track at two different places to test the dog's ability to stay with the original track. There will be at least two obstacles on the track, such as a change of cover, fences, creeks, ditches, etc. The dog must have a TD before entering a TDX. There is no certification required for a TDX.

Variable Surface Tracking—VST

This test came into effect in September 1995. The dog must have a TD earned at least six months prior to entering this test. The track is 600 to 800 yards long and shall have a minimum of 3 different surfaces. Vegetation shall be included along with two areas devoid of vegetation, such as concrete, asphalt, gravel, sand, hard pan, or mulch. The areas devoid of vegetation shall comprise at least one-third to one-half of the track. The track is aged three to five hours. There will be four to eight turns and four numbered articles, including one leather, one plastic, one metal, and one fabric dropped on the track. There is one starting flag. The handler will work at least 10 feet from the dog.

AGILITY

Agility was first introduced by John Varley at the Crufts Dog Show in England in February 1978, but Peter Meanwell, competitor and judge, actually developed the idea. It was officially recognized in the early '80s. Agility is extremely popular in England and Canada and growing in popularity in the US. The AKC

Agility has become a very popular canine sport and is one in which the Bernese Mountain Dog excels.

A well-trained and even-tempered Bernese Mountain Dog can participate in any activity, even playing in the snow.

acknowledged agility in August 1994. Dogs must be at least 12 months of age to be entered. It is a fascinating sport that the dog, handler, and spectators enjoy to the utmost. Agility is a spectator sport! The dog performs off lead. The handler either runs with his dog or positions himself on the course. He then directs his dog with verbal and hand signals over a timed course, over or through a variety of obstacles, including a time out or pause. One of the main drawbacks to agility is finding a place to train. The obstacles take up a lot of space, and it is very time consuming to put up and take down courses.

The titles earned at AKC agility trials are Novice Agility Dog (NAD), Open Agility Dog (OAD), Agility Dog Excellent (ADX), and Master Agility Excellent (MAX). In order to acquire an agility title, a dog must earn a qualifying score in his respective class on three separate occasions under two different judges. The MAX will be awarded after earning ten qualifying scores in the Agility Excellent Class.

PERFORMANCE TESTS

During the last decade, the American Kennel Club has promoted performance tests—those events that test the different breeds' natural abilities. This type of event encourages a handler to devote even more time to his dog and retain the natural instincts of his breed heritage. It is an important part of the wonderful world of dogs.

SCHUTZHUND

The German word "Schutzhund" translated to English means "protection dog." It is a fast-growing competitive sport in the United States and has been popular in England since the early 1900s. Schutzhund was originally a test to determine which German Shepherds were quality dogs for breeding in Germany. It gives us the ability to test dogs for correct temperament and working ability. Like every other dog sport, it requires teamwork between the handler and the dog.

Schutzhund training and showing involves three phases: tracking, obedience, and protection. There are three SchH levels: SchH I (novice), SchH II (intermediate), and SchH III (advanced). Each title becomes progressively more difficult. The handler and dog start out in each phase with 100 points. Points are deducted as errors are incurred. A total perfect score is 300, and for a dog and handler to earn a title he must earn at least 70 points in tracking and obedience and at least 80 points in protection. Today, many different breeds participate successfully in Schutzhund.

GENERAL INFORMATION

Obedience, tracking, and agility allow the purebred dog with an Indefinite Listing Privilege (ILP) number or a limited registration to be exhibited and earn titles. Application must be made to the AKC for an ILP number.

The American Kennel Club publishes *Events*, a monthly magazine that is part of the *Gazette*, their official journal for the sport of purebred dogs. The *Events* section lists upcoming shows and the secretary or superintendent for them. The majority of the conformation shows in the US are overseen by licensed superintendents. Generally, the entry closing date is approximately two-and-a-half weeks before the actual show. Point shows are fairly expensive, while the match shows cost about one-third of the point show entry fee. Match shows usually take entries the day of the show, but some are pre-entry. The best way to find match show information is through your local kennel club. Upon asking, the AKC can provide you with a list of superintendents, and you can write and ask to be put on their mailing lists.

Obedience trial and tracking test information is also available through the AKC. Frequently, these events are not superintended, but put on by the host club. Therefore, you would make the entry with the event's secretary.

There are numerous activities you can share with your dog. Regardless of what you do, it does take teamwork. Your dog can only benefit from your attention and training. We hope this chapter has enlightened you and hope, if nothing else, you will attend a show here and there. Perhaps you will start with a puppy kindergarten class, and who knows where it may lead!

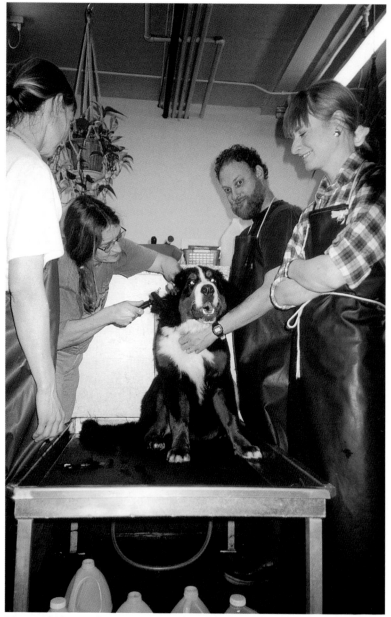

It's a good idea to take your Berner to the vet within 48 to 72 hours after acquiring him. He should also have regular checkups throughout his lifetime to maintain good health.

HEALTH CARE

Veterinary medicine has become far more sophisticated than what was available to our ancestors. This can be attributed to the increase in household pets and, consequently, the demand for better care for them. Also, human medicine has become far more complex. Today, diagnostic testing in veterinary medicine parallels human diagnostics. Because of better technology, we can expect our pets to live healthier lives, thereby increasing their life spans.

THE FIRST CHECKUP

You will want to take your new puppy/dog in for his first checkup within 48 to 72 hours after acquiring him. Many breeders strongly recommend this checkup and so do the humane shelters. A puppy/dog can appear healthy, but he may have a serious problem that is not apparent to the layman. Most pets have some type of a minor flaw that may never cause a real problem.

Unfortunately, if he should have a serious problem, you will want to consider the consequences of keeping the pet and the

Young puppies are very vulnerable to outside diseases. Responsible pet owners should take every precaution to keep their pups protected.

attachments that will be formed, which may be broken prematurely. Keep in mind there are many healthy dogs looking for good homes.

This first checkup is a good time to establish yourself with the veterinarian and to learn the office policy regarding their hours and how they handle emergencies. Usually, the breeder or another conscientious pet owner is a good reference for locating a capable veterinarian. You should be aware that not all vets give the same quality of service. Please do not make your selection based on the least expensive clinic, as they may be shortchanging your pet. There is the possibility that it will eventually cost you more due to improper diagnosis, treatment, etc. If you are selecting a new veterinarian, feel free to ask for a tour of the clinic. You should inquire about making an appointment for a tour, because all clinics are working clinics, and therefore, may not be available all day for sightseers. You may worry less if you see where your pet will be spending the day if he ever needs to be hospitalized.

The Physical Exam

Your veterinarian will check your pet's overall condition, which includes listening to the heart; checking the respiration; feeling the abdomen, muscles, and joints; checking the mouth, which includes gum color and signs of gum disease, along with plaque buildup; checking the ears for signs of an infection or ear mites; examining the eyes; and, last but not least, checking the condition of the skin and coat.

He should ask you questions regarding your pet's eating and elimination habits and invite you to relay your questions. It is a good idea to prepare a list so as not to forget anything. He should discuss the proper diet and the quantity to be fed. If this differs from your breeder's recommendation, you should convey to him what the breeder's choice is and see if he approves. If he recommends changing the diet, this should be done over a few days so as not to cause a gastrointestinal upset. It is customary to take in a fresh stool sample (just a small amount) to test for intestinal parasites. It must be fresh, preferably within 12 hours, because the eggs hatch quickly and after hatching will not be observed under the microscope. If your pet isn't obliging, the technician can usually take a sample in the clinic.

IMMUNIZATIONS

It is important that you take your puppy/dog's vaccination record with you on your first visit. In the case of a puppy, presumably the breeder has seen to the vaccinations up to the time you acquired custody. Veterinarians differ in their vaccination protocol. It is not unusual for your puppy to have received vaccinations for distemper, hepatitis, leptospirosis, parvovirus, and parainfluenza every two to three weeks from the age of five or six weeks. Usually, this is a combined injection and is typically called the DHLPP. The DHLPP is given through at least 12 to 14 weeks of age, and it is customary to continue with another parvovirus vaccine at 16 to 18 weeks. You may wonder why so many immunizations are necessary. No one knows for sure when the puppy's maternal antibodies are gone, although it is customarily accepted that distemper antibodies are gone by 12 weeks. Usually, parvovirus antibodies are gone by 16 to 18 weeks of age. However, it is possible for the maternal antibodies to be gone much earlier or even at a later age. Therefore, immunizations are started at an early age. The vaccine will not give immunity as long as there are maternal antibodies.

The rabies vaccination is given at three or six months of age, depending on your local laws. A vaccine for bordetella (kennel

A sudden change in your dog's behavior, such as sluggishness or loss of appetite, could indicate a health problem. Consult your vet if the condition persists.

cough) is advisable and can be given any time from the age of five weeks. The coronavirus is not commonly given unless there is a problem locally. The Lyme vaccine is necessary in endemic areas. Lyme disease has been reported in 47 states.

Distemper

Distemper is virtually an incurable disease. If the dog recovers, he is subject to severe nervous disorders. The virus attacks every tissue in the body and resembles a bad cold with a fever. It can cause a runny nose and eyes and cause gastrointestinal disorders, including a poor appetite, vomiting, and diarrhea. The virus is carried by raccoons, foxes, wolves, mink, and other dogs. Unvaccinated youngsters and senior citizens are very susceptible. This is still a common disease.

Hepatitis

Hepatitis is a virus that is most serious in very young dogs. It is spread by contact with an infected animal or its stool or urine. The virus affects the liver and kidneys and is characterized by high fever, depression, and lack of appetite. Recovered animals may be afflicted with chronic illnesses.

Leptospirosis

Leptospirosis is a bacterial disease transmitted by contact with the urine of an infected dog, rat, or other wildlife. It produces severe symptoms of fever, depression, jaundice, and internal bleeding and was fatal before the vaccine was developed. Recovered dogs can be carriers, and the disease can be transmitted from dogs to humans.

Parvovirus

Parvovirus was first noted in the late 1970s and is still a fatal disease. However, with proper vaccinations, early diagnosis, and prompt treatment, it is a manageable disease. It attacks the bone marrow and intestinal tract. The symptoms include depression, loss of appetite, vomiting, diarrhea, and collapse. Immediate medical attention is of the essence.

Rabies

Rabies is shed in the saliva and is carried by raccoons, skunks, foxes, other dogs, and cats. It attacks nerve tissue, resulting in

Bernese Mountain Dogs enjoy spending time outdoors. Be sure to take every precaution to prevent your dog from becoming infested with parasites.

paralysis and death. Rabies can be transmitted to people and is virtually always fatal. This disease is reappearing in the suburbs.

Bordetella (Kennel Cough)

The symptoms of bordetella are coughing, sneezing, hacking, and retching accompanied by nasal discharge usually lasting from a few days to several weeks. There are several disease-producing organisms responsible for this disease. The present vaccines are helpful but do not protect for all the strains. It usually is not life threatening, but in some instances it can progress to a serious bronchopneumonia. The disease is highly contagious. The vaccination should be given routinely for dogs that come into contact with other dogs, such as through boarding, training class, or visits to the groomer.

Coronavirus

Coronavirus is usually self-limiting and not a life-threatening disease. It was first noted in the late '70s about a year before parvovirus. The virus produces a yellow/brown stool, and there may be depression, vomiting, and diarrhea.

Maintaining your dog's immunization schedule and booster shots will help him live a long and healthy life.

Lyme Disease

Lyme disease was first diagnosed in the United States in 1976 in Lyme, CT, in people who lived in close proximity to the deer tick. Symptoms may include acute lameness, fever, swelling of joints, and loss of appetite. Your veterinarian can advise you if you live in an endemic area.

Booster Shots

After your puppy has completed his puppy vaccinations, you will continue to booster the DHLPP once a year. It is customary to booster the rabies one year after the first vaccine and then, depending on where you live, it should be boostered every year or every three years. This depends on your local laws. The Lyme and corona vaccines are boostered annually, and it is recommended that the bordetella be boostered every six to eight months.

ANNUAL VISIT

I would like to stress the importance of the annual checkup, which would include booster vaccinations, a check for intestinal parasites, and a test for heartworm. Today, in our very busy world, it is rush, rush, and see "how much you can get for how little." Unbelievably, some nonveterinary establishments have entered into the vaccination business. More harm than good can come to your dog through improper vaccinations, possibly from inferior vaccines and/or the wrong schedule. More than likely, you truly care about your companion dog, and over the years you have devoted much time and expense to his well being. Perhaps you are unaware that a vaccination is not just a vaccination. There is more involved. Please follow through with regular physical examinations. It is so important for your veterinarian to know your dog, and this is especially true during middle age and through the geriatric years. Your older dog may require more than one physical a year. The annual physical is good preventive medicine. Through early diagnosis and subsequent treatment, your dog can maintain a longer and better quality of life.

INTESTINAL PARASITES

Hookworms

Hookworms are almost microscopic intestinal worms that can cause anemia and, therefore, serious problems, including death, in

Puppies can acquire internal parasites, such as roundworms, while in the mother's uterus and through lactation. Careful breeding can increase the longevity of your puppy's life.

young puppies. Hookworms can be transmitted to humans through penetration of the skin. Puppies may be born with them.

Roundworms

Roundworms are spaghetti-like worms that can cause a potbellied appearance and dull coat, along with more severe symptoms such as vomiting, diarrhea, and coughing. Puppies acquire these while in the mother's uterus and through lactation. Both hookworms and roundworms may be acquired through ingestion.

Whipworms

Whipworms have a three-month life cycle and are not acquired through the dam. They cause intermittent diarrhea, usually with mucus. Whipworms are possibly the most difficult worm to eradicate. Their eggs are very resistant to most environmental factors and can last for years until the proper conditions enable them to mature. Whipworms are seldom seen in the stool.

Intestinal parasites are more prevalent in some areas than others. Climate, soil, and contamination are big factors contributing to the

Keeping your yard clean is the best preventative against worms. A fenced-in yard is also helpful in keeping stray and potentially infected dogs out of your Berner's area.

incidence of intestinal parasites. Eggs are passed in the stool, lay on the ground, and then become infective in a certain number of days. Each of the above worms has a different life cycle. Your dog's best chance of becoming and remaining worm-free is to always pooper-scoop your yard. A fenced-in yard keeps stray dogs out, which is certainly helpful.

Having a fecal examination done on your dog twice a year, or more often if there is a problem, is recommended. If your dog has a positive fecal sample, he will be given the appropriate medication and you will be asked to bring back another stool sample in a certain period of time (depending on the type of worm), and then he will be rewormed. This process goes on until he has at least two negative samples. Different types of worm require different medications. You will be wasting your money and doing your dog an injustice by buying over-the-counter medication without first consulting your veterinarian.

OTHER INTERNAL PARASITES

Coccidiosis and Giardiasis

Coccidiosis and giardiasis, which are protozoal infections, usually affect pups, especially in places where large numbers of puppies are brought together. Older dogs may harbor these infections, but do not show signs unless they are stressed. Symptoms include diarrhea, weight loss, and lack of appetite. These infections are not always apparent in the fecal examination.

Tapeworms

Seldom apparent on fecal floatation, tapeworms are diagnosed frequently as rice-like segments around the dog's anus and the base of the tail. Tapeworms are long, flat, and ribbon-like, sometimes several feet in length, and made up of many segments about five-eighths of an inch long. The two most common causes of tapeworm found in the dog are:
(1) The larval form of the flea tapeworm parasite matures in an intermediate host, the flea, before it can become infective. Your dog acquires this by ingesting the flea through licking and chewing.
(2) Rabbits, rodents, and certain large game animals serve as intermediate hosts for other species of tapeworm. If your dog eats one of these infected hosts, he can acquire tapeworms.

As your dog ages, his health needs will change. Keep veterinary visits regular and all vaccines up to date.

Heartworm Disease

Heartworm is a worm that resides in the heart and adjacent blood vessels of the lung that produces microfilaria, which circulate in the bloodstream. It is possible for a dog to be infected with any number of worms from one to a hundred that can be 6 to 14 inches long. It is a life-threatening disease, expensive to treat, and easily prevented. Depending on where you live, your veterinarian may recommend a preventive year-round and either an annual or semiannual blood test. The most common preventive is given once a month.

External Parasites

Fleas

Fleas are not only the dog's worst enemy, but also enemy to the owner's pocketbook. Preventing is less expensive than treating, but regardless, we'd prefer to spend our money elsewhere. Likely, the majority of our dogs are allergic to the bite of a flea, and in many cases, it only takes one flea bite. The protein in the flea's saliva is the culprit. Allergic dogs have a reaction, which usually results in a "hot spot." More than likely, such a reaction will involve a trip to the veterinarian for treatment. Yes, prevention is less expensive. Fortunately, today there are several good products available.

If there is a flea infestation, no one product is going to correct the problem. Not only will the dog require treatment, so will the environment. In general, flea collars are not very effective, although there is an "egg" collar now available that will kill the eggs on the dog. Dips are the most economical, but they are messy. There are some effective shampoos and treatments available through pet shops and veterinarians. An oral tablet arrived on the American market in 1995 and was popular in Europe the previous year. It sterilizes the female flea, but will not kill adult fleas. Therefore, the tablet, which is given monthly, will decrease the flea population but is not a "cure-all." Dogs that suffer from flea-bite allergy will still be subjected to the bite of the flea. Another popular parasiticide is permethrin, which is applied to the back of the dog in one or two places, depending on the dog's weight. This product works as a repellent, causing the flea to get "hot feet" and jump off. Do not confuse this product with some of the organophosphates that are also applied to the dog's back.

Some products are not usable on young puppies. Treating fleas should be done under your veterinarian's guidance. Frequently, it is necessary to combine products, and the layman does not have knowledge regarding possible toxicities. It is hard to believe, but there are a few dogs that do have a natural resistance to fleas. Nevertheless, it would be wise to treat all pets at the same time. Don't forget your cats. Cats just love to prowl the neighborhood, and, consequently, return with unwanted guests.

Adult fleas live on the dog, but their eggs drop off into the environment. There, they go through four larval stages before reaching adulthood, and thereby are able to jump back on the poor unsuspecting dog. The cycle resumes and takes between 21 to 28 days under ideal conditions. There are environmental products available that will kill both adult fleas and larvae.

Ticks

Ticks can carry Rocky Mountain Spotted Fever, Lyme disease, and can cause tick paralysis. They should be removed with tweezers. Try to pull out the head because the jaws carry disease. There is a tick preventive collar that does an excellent job. Ticks automatically back out on those dogs wearing collars.

Responsible breeders are dedicated to preserving and improving their breeds. Most breeders will ask that you have your dog spayed or neutered.

Sarcoptic Mange

Sarcoptic mange is a mite that is difficult to find on skin scrapings. The pinnal reflex is a good indicator of this disease. Rub the ends of the pinna (ear) together and the dog will start scratching with his foot. Sarcoptes are highly contagious to other dogs and to humans, although they do not live long on humans. They cause intense itching.

Demodectic Mange

Demodectic mange is a mite that is passed from the dam to her puppies. It commonly affects youngsters aged three to ten months. Diagnosis is confirmed by skin scraping. Small areas of alopecia around the eyes, lips, and/or forelegs become visible. There is little itching, unless there is a secondary bacterial infection. Some breeds are afflicted more than others.

Cheyletiella

Cheyletiella causes intense itching and is diagnosed by skin scraping. It lives in the outer layers of the skin of dogs, cats, rabbits, and humans. Yellow-gray scales may be found on the back and the rump, top of the head, and the nose.

TO BREED OR NOT TO BREED

More than likely, your breeder has requested that you have your puppy neutered or spayed. Your breeder's request is based on what is healthiest for your dog and what is most beneficial for your breed. Experienced and conscientious breeders devote many years to developing a bloodline. In order to do this, they make every effort to plan each breeding in regard to conformation, temperament, and health. This type of breeder does his best to perform the necessary testing (i.e., OFA, CERF, testing for inherited blood disorders, thyroid, etc.). Testing is expensive and sometimes very disheartening when a favorite dog doesn't pass his health tests. The health history pertains not only to the breeding stock, but to the immediate ancestors. Reputable breeders do not want their offspring to be bred indiscriminately. Therefore, you may be asked to neuter or spay your puppy. Of course, there is always the exception, and the breeder may agree to let you breed your dog under his direct supervision. This is an important concept. More and more effort is being made to breed healthier dogs.

Spaying or neutering your dog can greatly decrease his or her chances of developing reproductive complications.

Spay/Neuter

There are numerous benefits to spaying or neutering your dog at six months of age. Unspayed females are subject to mammary and ovarian cancer. In order to prevent mammary cancer, she must be spayed prior to her first heat cycle. Later in life, an unspayed female may develop a pyometra (an infected uterus), which is definitely life threatening.

Spaying is performed under a general anesthetic and is easy on the young dog. As you might expect, it is a little harder on the older dog, but that is no reason to deny her the surgery. The surgery removes the ovaries and uterus. It is important to remove all the ovarian tissue. If some is left behind, she could remain attractive to males. In order to view the ovaries, a reasonably long incision is necessary. An ovariohysterectomy is considered major surgery.

Neutering the male at a young age will inhibit some characteristic male behavior that owners frown upon. Some boys will not hike their legs and mark territory if they are neutered at six months of age. Also, neutering at a young age has hormonal benefits, lessening the chance of hormonal aggressiveness.

Surgery involves removing the testicles but leaving the scrotum. If there should be a retained testicle, the male definitely needs to be neutered before the age of two or three years. Retained testicles can develop cancer. Unneutered males are at risk for testicular cancer, perineal fistulas, perianal tumors and fistulas, and prostatic disease.

Intact males and females may be prone to housetraining accidents. Females urinate frequently before, during, and after heat cycles, and males tend to mark territory if there is a female in heat. Males may show the same behavior if there is a visiting dog or guests.

Surgery involves a sterile operating procedure equivalent to human surgery. The incision site is shaved, surgically scrubbed, and draped. The veterinarian wears a sterile surgical gown, cap, mask, and gloves. Anesthesia should be monitored by a registered technician. It is customary for the veterinarian to recommend a pre-anesthetic blood screening, looking for metabolic problems, and an ECG rhythm strip to check for normal heart function. Today, anesthetics are equal to human anesthetics, which enables your dog to walk out of the clinic the same day as surgery.

Some folks worry about their dogs gaining weight after being neutered or spayed. This is usually not the case. It is true that some dogs may be less active so they could develop a problem, but most

A shiny coat, clear bright eyes, and an energetic attitude are indications that your Bernese Mountain Dog is in proper condition.

are just as active as they were before surgery. However, if your dog should begin to gain, you need to decrease his food and see to it that he gets a little more exercise.

MEDICAL PROBLEMS

Anal Sacs

Anal sacs are small sacs on either side of the rectum that can cause the dog discomfort when they are full. They should empty when the dog has a bowel movement. Symptoms of inflammation or impaction are excessive licking under the tail and/or a bloody or sticky discharge from the anal area. Breeders recommend emptying the sacs on a regular schedule when bathing the dog. Many veterinarians prefer this isn't done unless there are symptoms. You can express the sacs by squeezing them (at the five and seven o'clock positions) in and up toward the anus. Take precautions not to get in the way of the foul-smelling fluid that is expressed. Some dogs object to this procedure, so it would be wise to have someone hold the head. Scooting is caused by anal-sac irritation and not worms.

Colitis

The stool may be frank blood or blood tinged and is the result of inflammation of the colon. Colitis, sometimes intermittent, can be the result of stress, undiagnosed whipworms, or perhaps idiopathic (no explainable reason). If intermittent bloody stools are an ongoing problem, you should probably feed a diet higher in fiber. Seek professional help if your dog feels poorly and/or the condition persists.

Conjunctivitis

Many breeds are prone to conjunctivitis. The conjunctiva is the pink tissue that lines the inner surface of the eyeball, except the clear, transparent cornea. Irritating substances such as bacteria, foreign matter, or chemicals can cause it to become reddened and swollen. It is important to keep any hair trimmed from around the eyes. Long hair stays damp and aggravates the problem. Keep the eyes cleaned with warm water and wipe away any matter that has accumulated in the corner of the eyes. If the condition persists, you should see your veterinarian. This problem goes hand in hand with keratoconjunctivitis sicca.

Ear Infection

Otitis externa is an inflammation of the external ear canal that begins at the outside opening of the ear and extends inward to the eardrum. Dogs with pendulous ears are prone to this disease, but breeds with upright ears also have a high incidence of problems. Allergies, food, and inhalents, along with hormonal problems, such as hypothyroidism, are major contributors to the disease. For those dogs that have recurring problems, you need to investigate the underlying causes if you hope to cure them.

Be careful never to get water in the ears. Water provides a great medium for bacteria to grow. If your dog swims or you inadvertently get water in his ears, use a drying agent. You can use an at-home preparation of equal parts of three-percent hydrogen peroxide and 70-percent rubbing alcohol. Another preparation is equal parts of white vinegar and water. Your veterinarian, alternatively, can provide a suitable product. When cleaning the ears, be careful using cotton tip applicators, because they make it easy to pack debris down into the canal. Only clean what you can see.

If your dog has an ongoing infection, don't be surprised if your veterinarian recommends sedating him and flushing his ears with a bulb syringe. Sometimes this needs to be done a few times to get the ear clean. The ear must be clean so that medication can come into contact with the canal. Be prepared to return for rechecks until the infection is gone. This may involve more flushings if the ears are very bad.

For chronic or recurring cases, your veterinarian may recommend thyroid testing, etc., and a hypoallergenic diet for a trial period of 10 to 12 weeks. Depending on your dog, it may be a good idea to see a dermatologist. Ears shouldn't be taken lightly. If the condition gets out of hand, surgery may be necessary. Please ask your veterinarian to explain proper ear maintenance for your dog.

Flea Bite Allergy

Flea bite allergy is the result of a hypersensitivity to the bite of a flea and its saliva. It only takes one bite to cause the dog to chew or scratch himself raw. Your dog may need medical attention to ease his discomfort. You need to clip the hair around the "hot spot" and wash it with a mild soap and water, and you may need to do this daily if the area weeps. Apply an antibiotic anti-inflammatory product. Hot spots can occur from other trauma, such as grooming.

All dogs have off days when they do not seem themselves. However, if this lethargic condition persists, you should have your Berner examined by a professional.

Interdigital Cysts

Check for interdigital cysts on your dog's feet if he shows signs of lameness. They are frequently associated with staph infections and can be quite painful. A home remedy is to soak the infected foot in a solution of a half teaspoon of bleach in a couple of quarts of water. Do this two to three times a day for a couple of days. Check with your veterinarian for an alternative remedy; antibiotics usually work well. If there is a recurring problem, surgery may be required.

Lameness

Lameness may only be an interdigital cyst or it could be a mat between the toes, especially if your dog licks his feet. Sometimes it is hard to determine which leg is affected. If your dog is holding up his leg, you need to see your veterinarian.

Skin

Frequently, poor skin is the result of an allergy to fleas, inhalants, or food. These types of problems usually result in a staph dermatitis. Dogs with food allergies usually show signs of severe itching and scratching. Some dogs with food allergies never once itch. Their only symptom is swelling of the ears with no ear infection. Food allergy may result in recurrent bacterial skin and ear infections. Your veterinarian or dermatologist will recommend a good restricted diet. It is not wise for you to hit and miss with different dog foods. Many of the diets offered over the counter are not the hypoallergenic diets you are led to believe. Dogs acquire allergies through exposure.

Inhalant allergies result in atopy, which causes licking of the feet, scratching the body, and rubbing the muzzle. They may be seasonable. Your veterinarian or dermatologist can perform intradermal testing for inhalant allergies. If your dog should test positive, then a vaccine may be prepared. The results are very satisfying.

Tonsillitis

Usually, young dogs have a higher incidence of tonsillitis than the older ones. Older dogs have built up resistance. It is very contagious. Sometimes it is difficult to determine if the condition is tonsillitis or kennel cough because the symptoms are similar. Symptoms include fever, poor eating, swallowing with difficulty, and retching up a white, frothy mucus.

DENTAL CARE for Your Dog's Life

S o, you have a new puppy! Anyone who has ever raised a puppy is abundantly aware of how this new arrival affects the household. Your puppy will chew anything he can reach, chase your shoelaces, and play "tear the rag" with any piece of clothing he can find. When puppies are newly born, they have no teeth. At about four weeks of age, puppies of most breeds begin to develop their deciduous or baby teeth. They begin eating semi-solid food, biting and fighting with their littermates, and learning discipline from their mother. As their new teeth come in, they inflict pain on their mother's breasts, so feeding sessions become less frequent and shorter. By six or eight weeks, the mother will start growling to warn her pups when they are fighting too roughly or hurting her as they nurse too much with their new teeth.

Puppies need to chew. It is a necessary part of their physical and mental development. They develop muscles and necessary life skills as they drag objects around, fight over possession, and vocalize alerts and warnings. Puppies chew on things to explore their world. They are using their sense of taste to determine what is food and what is not. How else can they tell an electrical cord from a lizard? At about four months of age, most puppies begin shedding their baby teeth. Often, these teeth need some help to come out to make way for the permanent teeth. The incisors (front teeth) will be replaced first. Then, the adult canine or fang teeth erupt. When a baby tooth is not shed before the permanent tooth comes in, veterinarians call it a

All puppies need to chew as part of their physical and mental development.

Providing your dog with safe chew toys, such as a Nylabone®, will keep him occupied and maintain good oral care.

retained deciduous tooth. This condition will often cause gum infections by trapping hair and debris between the permanent tooth and the retained baby tooth. Puppies that are given adequate chew toys will exhibit less destructive behavior, develop more physically, and have less chance of retained deciduous teeth.

During the first year, your dog should be seen by your veterinarian at regular intervals. He will let you know when to bring your puppy in for vaccinations and parasite examinations. At each visit, your vet should inspect the lips, teeth, and mouth as part of a complete physical examination. You should take some part in the maintenance of your dog's oral health. Examine your dog's mouth weekly throughout his first year to make sure there are no sores, foreign objects, tooth problems, etc. If your dog drools excessively, shakes his head, or has bad breath, consult your veterinarian. By the time your dog is six months old, his permanent teeth are all in and plaque can start to accumulate on the tooth surfaces. This is when your dog needs good dental-care habits to prevent calculus buildup on his teeth. Brushing is best—that is a fact that cannot be denied. However, some dogs do not like their teeth brushed regularly, or you may not be able to accomplish the task. In this case, you should consider a product that will help prevent plaque and calculus

Your dog's oral care is just as important as his grooming or nutritional needs. Have his teeth checked once a year by your vet.

buildup, like any of the dental devices available from Nylabone®.

By the time dogs are four years old, 75 percent of them have periodontal disease. It is the most common infection in dogs. Yearly examinations by your vet are essential to maintaining your dog's good health. If he detects periodontal disease, he or she may recommend a prophylactic cleaning. To do a thorough cleaning, it will be necessary to put your dog under anesthesia. With modern gas anesthetics and monitoring equipment, the procedure is pretty safe. Your veterinarian will scale the teeth with an ultrasound scaler or hand instrument. This removes the calculus from the teeth. If there are calculus deposits below the gum line, the veterinarian will plane the roots to make them smooth. After all of the calculus has been removed, the teeth are polished with pumice in a polishing cup. If any medical or surgical treatment is needed, it is done at this time. The final step would be fluoride treatment and your follow-up treatment at home. If the periodontal disease is advanced, the veterinarian may prescribe a medicated mouth rinse or antibiotics for use at home. Make sure your dog has safe, clean, and attractive chew toys, like Nylabones®, and healthy treats.

As your dog ages, professional examination and cleaning should become more frequent. The mouth should be inspected at least once a year. Your vet may recommend visits every six months. In the geriatric patient, organs such as the heart, liver, and kidneys do not function as well as when your dog was young. Your vet will probably want to test these organs' functions prior to using general anesthesia for dental cleaning. If your dog is a good chewer and you work closely with your vet, he can keep all of his teeth all of his life. However, as your dog ages, his sense of smell, sight, and taste will diminish. He may not have the desire to chase, trap, or chew his toys. He will also not have the energy to chew for long periods, as arthritis and periodontal disease could make chewing painful. This will leave you with more responsibility for keeping his teeth clean and healthy. The dog that would not let you brush his teeth at one year of age, may let you brush his teeth now that he is ten years old.

If you train your dog with good chewing habits as a puppy, he will have healthier teeth throughout his life.

TRAVELING With Your Dog

The earlier you start traveling with your new puppy or dog, the better. He needs to become accustomed to traveling. However, some dogs are nervous riders and become carsick easily. It is helpful if he starts any trip with an empty stomach. Do not despair, as it will go better if you continue taking him with you on short, fun rides. How would you feel if every time you rode in the car you stopped at the doctor's office for an injection? You would soon dread that nasty car. Older dogs that tend to get carsick may have more of a problem adjusting to traveling. Those dogs that are having serious problems may benefit from medication prescribed by the veterinarian.

Do give your dog a chance to relieve himself before getting into the car. It is a good idea to be prepared for a clean up with a leash, paper towels, bag, and terry cloth towel.

When in the car, the safest place for your dog is in a fiberglass or wire crate, although close confinement can promote carsickness in some dogs.

Your Berner puppy needs to become accustomed to traveling in the car as soon as possible. Make sure that your dog is secure in a crate, such as the Nylabone® Fold-Away Pet Carrier.

An alternative to the crate would be to use a car harness made for dogs and/or a safety strap attached to the harness or collar. Whatever you do, do not let your dog ride in the back of a pickup truck unless he is securely tied on a very short lead. I've seen trucks stop quickly, and, even though the dog was tied, he fell out and was dragged.

Another advantage of the crate is that it is a safe place to leave your dog if you need to run into the store. Otherwise, you wouldn't be able to leave the windows down. Keep in mind that while many dogs are overly protective in their crates, this may not be enough to deter dognappers. In some states, it is against the law to leave a dog in the car unattended.

Never leave a dog loose in the car wearing a collar and leash. More than one dog has killed himself by hanging. Do not let him put his head out an open window. Foreign debris can be blown into his eyes. When leaving your dog unattended in a car, consider the temperature. It can take less than five minutes to reach temperatures over 100°.

TRIPS

Perhaps you are taking a trip. Give consideration to what is best for your dog—traveling with you or boarding. When traveling by car, van, or motor home, you need to think ahead about locking your vehicle. In all probability you have many valuables in the car and do not wish to leave it unlocked. Perhaps most valuable and not replaceable is your dog. Give thought to securing your vehicle and providing adequate ventilation for him. Another consideration for you when traveling with your dog is medical problems that may arise and little inconveniences, such as exposure to external parasites. Some areas of the country are quite flea infested. You may want to carry flea spray with you. This is even a good idea when staying in motels. Quite possibly you are not the only occupants of the room.

Unbelievably, many motels and even hotels do allow canine guests, even some very first-class ones. Gaines Pet Foods Corporation publishes *Touring With Towser*, a directory of domestic hotels and motels that accommodate guests with dogs. Their address is Gaines TWT, PO Box 5700, Kankakee, IL, 60902. Call ahead to any motel that you may be considering and see if they accept pets. Sometimes it is necessary to pay a deposit against room damage. The management may feel reassured if you mention that your dog will be crated. If you do travel with your dog, take along plenty of baggies so that you can

It's not a good idea to leave your dog in the car on a warm day. If your Berner can't accompany you, leave him at home where he'll be comfortable.

clean up after him. When we all do our share in cleaning up, we make it possible for motels to continue accepting our pets. As a matter of fact, you should practice cleaning up everywhere you take your dog.

Depending on where your are traveling, you may need an up-to-date health certificate issued by your veterinarian. It is good policy to take along your dog's medical information, which would include the name, address, and phone number of your veterinarian, vaccination record, rabies certificate, and any medication he is taking.

AIR TRAVEL

When traveling by air, you need to contact the airlines to check their policy. Usually, you have to make arrangements up to a couple of weeks in advance when traveling with your dog. The airlines require your dog to travel in an airline-approved fiberglass crate. These can be purchased through the airlines, but they are also readily available in most pet-supply stores. If your dog is not accustomed to a crate, it is a good idea to get him acclimated to it before your trip.

The day of the actual trip you should withhold water about 1 hour ahead of departure and food for about 12 hours. The airlines generally have temperature restrictions that do not allow pets to travel if it is either too cold or too hot. Frequently, these restrictions are based on the temperatures at the departure and arrival airports. It's best to inquire about a health certificate. These usually need to be issued within ten days of departure. You should arrange for nonstop, direct flights, and if a commuter plane is involved, check to see if it will carry dogs. Some don't. The Humane Society of the United States has put together a tip sheet for airline traveling. You can receive a copy by sending a self-addressed, stamped envelope to:

The Humane Society of the United States
Tip Sheet
2100 L Street NW
Washington, DC 20037.

Regulations differ for traveling outside of the country and are sometimes changed without notice. Well in advance of your trip you need to write or call the appropriate consulate or agricultural department for instructions. Some countries have lengthy quarantines

Before putting your Bernese Mountain Dog in a boarding kennel, visit the facilities to make sure that they are clean and run efficiently.

(six months), and many differ in their rabies vaccination requirements. For instance, it may have to be given at least 30 days ahead of your departure.

Do make sure your dog is wearing proper identification including your name, phone number, and city. You never know when you might be in an accident and separated from your dog, or your dog could be frightened and somehow manage to escape and run away.

Another suggestion would be to carry in-case-of-emergency instructions. These would include the address and phone number of a relative or friend, your veterinarian's name, address, and phone number, and your dog's medical information.

BOARDING KENNELS

Perhaps you have decided that you need to board your dog. Your veterinarian can recommend a good boarding facility or possibly a pet sitter that will come to your house. It is customary for the boarding kennel to ask for proof of vaccination for the DHLPP, rabies, and bordetella vaccines. The bordetella should have been given within six months of boarding. This is for your protection. If they do not ask for this proof, I would not board at their kennel. Ask about flea control. Those dogs that suffer flea-bite allergy can get in trouble at a boarding kennel. Unfortunately, boarding kennels are limited as to how much they are able to do.

For more information on pet sitting, contact NAPPS:
National Association of Professional Pet Sitters
1200 G Street, NW
Suite 760
Washington, DC 20005.

Some pet clinics have technicians that pet sit and that board clinic patients in their homes. This may be an alternative for you. Ask your veterinarian if they have an employee that can help you. There is a definite advantage to having a technician care for your dog, especially if he is on medication or is a senior citizen.

You can write to the ASPCA for a copy of *Traveling With Your Pet:* ASPCA, Education Department, 441 E. 92nd Street, New York, NY 10128.

IDENTIFICATION and Finding the Lost Dog

There are several ways of identifying your dog. The old standby is a collar with dog license, rabies, and ID tags. Unfortunately, collars have a way of being separated from dogs and tags fall off. We're not suggesting you shouldn't use a collar and tags. If they stay intact and on the dog, they are the quickest form of identification.

For several years, owners have been tattooing their dogs. Some tattoos use a number with a registry. Herein lies the problem, because there are several registries to check. If you wish to tattoo your dog, use your social security number. Humane shelters have the means to trace it. It is usually done on the inside of the rear thigh. The area is first shaved and numbed. There is no pain, although some dogs do not like the buzzing sound. Occasionally, tattooing is not legible and needs to be redone.

The newest method of identification is microchipping. The microchip is a computer chip that is no larger than a grain of rice. The veterinarian implants it by injection between the shoulder blades. The dog feels no discomfort. If your dog is lost and picked up by the humane society, they can trace you by scanning the microchip, which has its own code. Most microchip scanners are

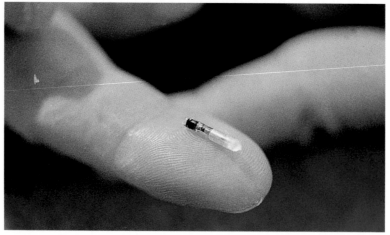

The newest method of identification is the microchip, which is a computer chip no bigger than a grain of rice that can help you track your dog's whereabouts.

friendly to other brands of microchips and their registries. The microchip comes with a dog tag saying that the dog is microchipped. It is the safest way of identifying your dog.

FINDING THE LOST DOG

Most people would agree that there would be little worse than losing your dog. Responsible pet owners rarely lose their dogs. They do not let their dogs run free because they don't want harm to come to them. Not only that, but in most if not all states, there is a leash law.

Beware of fenced-in yards. They can be a hazard. Dogs find ways to escape either over or under fences. Another fast exit may be through the gate that perhaps someone left unlocked.

Below is a list that will hopefully be of help to you if you lose your pet. Remember, don't give up, keep looking. Your dog is worth your efforts.

1. Contact your neighbors and put flyers with a photo on it in their mailboxes. Information you should include would be the dog's name, breed, sex, color, age, source of identification, when your dog was last seen and where, and your name and phone numbers. It may be helpful to say that the dog needs medical care. Offer a *reward*.

2. Check all local shelters daily. It is also possible for your dog to be picked up away from home and end up in an out-of-the-way shelter. Check these, too. Go in person. It is not enough to call. Most shelters are limited on the time they can hold dogs before they are put up for adoption or euthanized. There is the possibility that your dog will not make it to the shelter for several days. He could have been wandering or someone may have tried to keep him.

3. Notify all local veterinarians. Call and send flyers.

4. Call your breeder. Frequently, breeders are contacted when one of their breed is found.

5. Contact the rescue group for your breed.

6. Contact local schools—children may have seen your dog.

7. Post flyers at the schools, groceries, gas stations, convenience stores, veterinary clinics, groomers, and any other places that will allow them.

8. Advertise in the newspaper.

9. Advertise on the radio.

BEHAVIOR and Canine Communication

Studies of the human/animal bond point out the importance of the unique relationships that exist between people and their pets. Those of us who share our lives with pets understand the special part they play through companionship, service, and protection. For many, the pet/owner bond goes beyond simple companionship; pets are often considered members of the family. A leading pet food manufacturer recently conducted a nationwide survey of pet owners to gauge just how important pets were in their lives. Here's what they found:

- 76 percent allow their pets to sleep on their beds
- 78 percent think of their pets as their children
- 84 percent display photos of their pets, mostly in their homes
- 84 percent think that their pets react to their own emotions
- 100 percent talk to their pets
- 97 percent think that their pets understand what they're saying

Are you surprised?

Senior citizens show more concern for their own eating habits when they have the responsibility of feeding a dog. Seeing that their dogs are

The bond between humans and animals is a strong one. It's proven that pets help to relieve stress and lessen the occurrence of illness in their owners.

Pets need to feel like they are an integral part of their families' lives. Do your best to provide a loving and stimulating environment for your Bernese Mountain Dog.

routinely exercised encourages the owners to think of schedules that otherwise may seem unimportant to a senior citizen. The older owner may be arthritic and feeling poorly, but with responsibility for his dog he has a reason to get up and get moving. It is a big plus if his dog is an attention seeker that will demand such from his owner.

Over the last couple of decades, it has been shown that pets relieve the stress of those who lead busy lives. Owning a pet has been known to lessen the occurrence of heart attack and stroke.

Many single folks thrive on the companionship of their dogs. Lifestyles are very different from a long time ago, and today more individuals seek the single life. However, they receive fulfillment from owning dogs.

Most likely, the majority of dogs live in family environments. The companionship they provide is well worth the effort involved. In my opinion, every child should have the opportunity to have a family dog. Dogs teach responsibility through the understanding of their care, feelings, and even respect for their life cycles. Frequently, those children who have not been exposed to dogs grow up afraid of them, which isn't good. Dogs sense timidity, and some will take advantage of the situation.

Today, more dogs are working as service dogs. Since the origination of the Seeing Eye dogs years ago, we now have dogs trained to aid the deaf. Also, dogs are trained to provide service for the handicapped and are able to perform many different tasks for their owners. Search and rescue dogs, with their handlers, are sent throughout the world to assist in the recovery of disaster victims. They are lifesavers.

Therapy dogs are very popular with nursing homes, and some hospitals even allow them to visit. The inhabitants truly look forward to their visits. They wanted and were allowed to have visiting dogs to hold and love.

Nationally, there is a Pet Awareness Week to educate students and others about the value and basic care of our pets. Many countries take an even greater interest in their pets than Americans do. In those countries, pets are allowed to accompany their owners into restaurants and shops, etc. In the US, this freedom is only available to our service dogs. Even so, we think very highly of the human/animal bond.

CANINE BEHAVIOR

Canine behavior problems are the number-one reason that pet owners dispose of their dogs, either through new homes, humane

Learning how a dog communicates will help you to better understand certain behaviors.

shelters, or euthanasia. Unfortunately, there are too many owners who are unwilling to devote the necessary time to properly train their dogs. On the other hand, there are those who are not only concerned about inherited health problems but are also aware of the dog's mental stability.

You may realize that a breed and his group relatives (i.e., sporting, hounds, etc.) show tendencies toward behavioral characteristics. An experienced breeder can acquaint you with his breed's personality. Unfortunately, many breeds are labeled with poor temperaments, when actually the breed as a whole is not affected but rather only a small percentage of individuals within the breed.

Inheritance and environment contribute to the dog's behavior. Some naïve people suggest inbreeding as the cause of bad temperaments. Inbreeding only results in poor behavior if the ancestors carry the trait. If there are excellent temperaments behind the dogs, then good breeding practices will promote good temperaments in the offspring. Did you ever consider that inbreeding is what sets the characteristics of a breed? A purebred dog is the end result of inbreeding. This does not spare the mixed-breed dog from the same problems. Mixed-breed dogs are frequently the offspring of purebred dogs.

Not too many decades ago most dogs led a different lifestyle than what is prevalent today. Usually, mom stayed home, so the dog had human companionship and someone to discipline him if needed. Not much was expected from the family pet. Today's mom works, and everyone's life is at a much faster pace.

The dog may have to adjust to being a "weekend" dog. The family is gone all day during the week, and he is left to his own devices for entertainment. Some dogs sleep all day waiting for their families to come home, and others become wigwam wreckers if given the opportunity. Crates do ensure the safety of the dog and the house. However, he could become physically and emotionally crippled if he doesn't get enough exercise and attention. We still appreciate and want the companionship of our dogs, although we expect more from them. In many cases, we tend to forget dogs are just that—*dogs'* not human beings.

SOCIALIZING AND TRAINING

Many prospective puppy buyers lack experience regarding the proper socialization and training needed to develop the type of pets we all desire. In the first 18 months, training does take some work. It is easier to start proper training before there is a problem that needs to be corrected.

The initial work begins with the breeder. The breeder should start socializing the puppy at five to six weeks of age and cannot let up.

Introducing your puppy to new people, places, and experiences will help him to become a confident and well-socialized adult dog.

Providing your Bernese Mountain Dog with the proper training and socialization early in life will help prevent behavioral problems.

Human socializing is critical up through 12 weeks of age and is likewise important during the following months. The litter should be left together during the first few weeks, but it is necessary to separate the pups by ten weeks of age. Leaving them together after that time will increase competition for litter dominance. If puppies are not socialized with people by 12 weeks of age, they will be timid in later life.

The eight- to ten-week age period can be a fearful time for puppies. They need to be handled very gently by children and adults. There should be no harsh discipline during this time. Starting at 14 weeks of age, the puppy begins the juvenile period, which ends when he reaches sexual maturity around 6 to 14 months of age. During the juvenile period, he needs to be introduced to strangers (adults, children, and other dogs) on the home property. At sexual maturity, he will begin to bark at strangers and become more protective. Males start to lift their legs to urinate, but you can inhibit this behavior by walking your boy on leash away from trees, shrubs, fences, etc.

Perhaps you are thinking about getting an older puppy. You need to inquire about the puppy's social experience. If he has lived in a kennel, he may have a hard time adjusting to people and environmental stimuli. Assuming he has had a good social upbringing, there are advantages to an older puppy.

Training includes puppy kindergarten and a minimum of one to two basic training classes. During these classes, you will learn how to train your youngster. This is especially important if you own a large breed of dog. It is somewhat harder, if not nearly impossible, for some owners to be the alpha figure when their dog reaches adult size. You will be taught how to properly restrain your dog. This concept is important. Again, it puts you in the alpha position. All dogs need to be restrained many times during their lives. Believe it or not, some of the worst offenders are the eight-week-old puppies that are brought to our clinic. They need to be gently restrained for a nail trim, but the way they carry on you would think we were killing them. In comparison, their vaccination is a "piece of cake." When we ask dogs to do something that is not agreeable to them, their worst comes out. Life will be easier for your dog if you expose him at a young age to the necessities of life—proper behavior and restraint.

Understanding the Dog's Language

Most authorities agree that the dog is a descendent of the wolf. The dog and the wolf have similar traits. For instance both are pack oriented and prefer not to be isolated for long periods of time. Another characteristic is that the dog, like the wolf, looks to the leader—alpha—for direction. Both the wolf and the dog communicate through body language, not only within their packs but with outsiders.

Every pack has an alpha figure. The dog looks to you, or should look to you, to be that leader. If your dog doesn't receive the proper training and guidance, he very well may replace you as alpha. This would be a serious problem and is certainly a disservice to your dog.

Eye contact is one way the alpha wolf keeps order within his pack. You are alpha so you must establish eye contact with your puppy. Obviously, your puppy will have to look at you. Practice eye contact, even if you need to hold his head for five to ten seconds at a time. You can give him a treat as a reward. Make sure your eye contact is gentle and not threatening. Later, if he has been naughty, it is permissible to give him a long, penetrating look. There are some older dogs that never learned eye contact as puppies and cannot accept eye contact. You should avoid eye contact with these dogs since they feel threatened and will retaliate as such.

Your Bernese Mountain Dog should look to you as his leader, or Alpha. Establishing gentle eye contact with him will let you know that you are in charge.

BODY LANGUAGE

The play bow, when the forequarters are down and the hindquarters are elevated, is an invitation to play. Puppies play fight, which helps them learn the acceptable limits of biting. This is necessary later in their lives. Nevertheless, an owner may be falsely reassured by the playful nature of his dog's aggression. Playful aggression toward another dog or human may be an indication of serious aggression in the future. Owners should never play fight or play tug-of-war with any dog that is inclined to be dominant.

Signs of submission are:

1. Avoids eye contact.
2. Active submission—the dog crouches down, ears back and tail lowered.
3. Passive submission—the dog rolls on his side, with his hindlegs in the air, and frequently urinates.

Signs of dominance are:

1. Makes eye contact.
2. Stands with ears up, tail up, and the hair raised on his neck.
3. Shows dominance over another dog by standing at right angles over him.

A dog's body language can tell you a lot about his personality. These Berners look happy and relaxed.

Dominant dogs tend to behave in characteristic ways such as:

1. The dog may be unwilling to move from his place (i.e., reluctant to give up the sofa if the owner wants to sit there).

2. He may not part with toys or objects in his mouth and may show possessiveness with his food bowl.

3. He may not respond quickly to commands.

4. He may be disagreeable for grooming and dislikes being petted.

Dogs are popular because of their sociable nature. Those that have contact with humans during the first 12 weeks of life regard them as a member of their own species—their pack. All dogs have the potential for both dominant and submissive behavior. Only through experience and training do they learn to whom it is appropriate to show which behavior. Not all dogs are concerned with dominance, but owners need to be aware of that potential. It is wise for the owner to establish his dominance early on.

A human can express dominance or submission toward a dog in the following ways:

1. Meeting the dog's gaze signals dominance. Averting the gaze signals submission. If the dog growls or threatens, averting the gaze is the first avoiding action to take—it may prevent attack. It is important to establish eye contact in the puppy. The older dog that has not been exposed to eye contact may see it as a threat and will not be willing to submit.

The Bernese Mountain Dog has an amazing capacity to learn. With the correct approach and guidance, you can train your dog to be an excellent canine citizen.

2. Being above the dog signals dominance; being lower signals submission. This is why, when attempting to make friends with a strange dog or catch the runaway, one should kneel down to his level. Some owners see their dogs become dominant when allowed on the furniture or on the bed. Then the dog is at the owner's level.

3. An owner can gain dominance by ignoring all the dog's social initiatives. The owner pays attention to the dog only when he obeys a command.

No dog should be allowed to achieve dominant status over any adult or child. Ways of preventing this are as follows:

1. Handle the puppy gently, especially during the three- to four-month period.

2. Let the children and adults hand-feed him and teach him to take food without lunging or grabbing.

3. Do not allow him to chase children or joggers.

4. Do not allow him to jump on people or mount their legs. Even females may be inclined to mount. It is not only a male habit.

5. Do not allow him to growl for any reason.

6. Don't participate in wrestling or tug-of-war games.

7. Don't physically punish a puppy for aggressive behavior. Restrain him from repeating the infraction and teach an alternative behavior. Dogs should earn everything they receive from their owners. This would include sitting to receive petting or treats, sitting before going out the door, and sitting to receive the collar and leash. These types of exercises reinforce the owner's dominance.

Young children should never be left alone with a dog. It is important that children learn some basic obedience commands so they have some control over the dog. They will gain his respect.

FEAR

One of the most common problems dogs can experience is being fearful. Some dogs are more afraid than others. On the lesser side, which is sometimes humorous to watch, dogs can be afraid of a strange object. They act silly when something is out of place in the house. We call this trait perceptive intelligence. He realizes the abnormal within his known environment. He does not react the same way in strange environments since he does not know what is normal.

If your dog is acting fearful of a situation or object, try not to dwell on his fright. Instead, direct his attention to something else.

On the more serious side is a fear of people. This can result in backing off, seeking his own space and saying "leave me alone," or it can result in an aggressive behavior that may lead to challenging the person. Respect that the dog wants to be left alone and give him time to come forward. If you approach the cornered dog, he may resort to snapping. If you leave him alone, he may decide to come forward, which should be rewarded with a treat.

Some dogs may initially be too fearful to take treats. In these cases it is helpful to make sure the dog hasn't eaten for about 24 hours. Being a little hungry encourages him to accept the treats, especially if they are of the "gourmet" variety.

Dogs can be afraid of numerous things, including loud noises and thunderstorms. Invariably, the owner rewards (by comforting) the dog when he shows signs of fearfulness. When your dog is frightened, direct his attention to something else. Don't dwell on his fright.

AGGRESSION

Some different types of aggression are: predatory, defensive, dominance, possessive, protective, fear induced, noise provoked, "rage"

If your dog is behaving aggressively, have him perform a simple command, like the sit, which immediately puts you in a dominant position.

syndrome (unprovoked aggression), maternal, and aggression directed toward other dogs. Aggression is the most common behavioral problem encountered. Protective breeds are expected to be more aggressive than others, but with the proper upbringing they can make very dependable companions. You need to be able to read your dog.

Many factors contribute to aggression, including genetics and environment. An improper environment, which may include living conditions, lack of social life, excessive punishment, being attacked or frightened by an aggressive dog, etc., can all influence a dog's behavior. Even spoiling him and giving too much praise may be detrimental. Isolation and the lack of human contact or exposure to frequent teasing by children or adults also can ruin a good dog.

Lack of direction, fear, or confusion lead to aggression in those dogs that are so inclined. Any obedience exercise, even the sit and down, can direct the dog and overcome his fear and/or confusion. Every dog should learn these commands as a youngster, and there should be periodic reinforcement.

When a dog is showing signs of aggression, you should speak calmly (no screaming or hysterics) and firmly give a command that he understands, such as the sit. As soon as your dog obeys, you have assumed your dominant position. Aggression presents a problem because there may be danger to others. Sometimes it is an emotional issue. Owners may consciously or unconsciously encourage their dogs' aggression. Other owners show responsibility by accepting the problem and taking measures to keep it under control. The owner is responsible for his dog's actions, and it is not wise to take a chance on someone being bitten, especially a child. Euthanasia is the solution for some owners, and in severe cases this may be the best choice. However, few dogs are that dangerous and very few are that much of a threat to their owners. If caution is exercised and professional help is gained early on, most cases can be controlled.

Some authorities recommend feeding a lower protein (less than 20 percent) diet. They believe this can aid in reducing aggression. If the dog loses weight, vegetable oil can be added. Veterinarians and behaviorists are having some success with pharmacology. In many cases, treatment is possible and can improve the situation.

If you have done everything according to "the book" regarding training and socializing and are still having a behavior problem, don't procrastinate. It is important that the problem gets attention before it is out of hand. It is estimated that 20 percent of a veterinarian's time may be devoted to dealing with problems before they become so intolerable that the dog is separated from his home and owner. If your veterinarian isn't able to help, he can refer you to a behaviorist.

Problems

Barking
Barking is a habit that shouldn't be encouraged. Some owners desire their dogs to bark so as to be watchdogs. Most dogs will bark when a stranger comes to the door.

The new puppy frequently barks or whines in the crate in his strange, unfamiliar environment, and the owner reinforces the puppy's bad behavior by going to him during the night. This is a no-no. Smack the top of the crate and say, "Quiet," in a loud, firm voice. Puppies don't like to hear the loud noise of a crate being banged. If the barking is sleep-interrupting, the owner should take crate and pup to the bedroom for a few days until the puppy becomes adjusted to his new environment. Otherwise, ignore the barking during the night.

Barking can be a breed trait or a bad habit learned through the environment. It takes dedication to stop the barking. Attention should be paid to the cause of it. Does the dog seek attention, does he need to go out, is it feeding time, is it occurring when he is left alone, is it a protective bark, etc.? Overzealous barking can be a breed tendency. When barking presents a problem for you, try to stop it as soon as it begins.

There are electronic collars available that are supposed to curb barking. There are some disadvantages to the collar. If the dog is barking out of excitement, punishment is not the appropriate treatment. Presumably, there is the chance the collar could be activated by other stimuli and thereby punish the dog when he is not barking. If you decide to use one, you should seek help from a person with experience with that type of collar. Nevertheless, the root of the problem needs to be investigated and corrected.

In extreme circumstances (usually when there is a problem with the neighbors), some people have resorted to having their dogs debarked. Be cautioned that the dog continues to bark, but usually only a squeaking sound is heard. Frequently, the vocal cords grow back. Probably the biggest concern is that the dog can be left with scar tissue, which can narrow the opening to the trachea.

Jumping Up

A dog that jumps up is a happy dog. Nevertheless, few guests appreciate dogs jumping on them. Clothes get footprinted and/or snagged.

Some trainers believe in allowing the puppy to jump up during his first few weeks. If you correct him too soon and at the wrong age, you may intimidate him. Consequently, he could be timid around humans later in his life. However, there will come a time, probably around four months of age, that he needs to know when it is okay to jump and when he is to show off good manners by sitting instead.

Some authorities never allow jumping. If you are irritated by your dog jumping up on you, then you should discourage it from the beginning. A larger breed of dog can cause harm to a senior citizen. Some are quite fragile. It may not take much to cause a topple that could break a hip.

How do you correct the problem? All family members need to participate in teaching the puppy to sit as soon as he starts to jump up. The sit must be practiced every time he does it. Don't forget to praise him for his good behavior. If an older dog has acquired the habit, grasp his paws and squeeze tightly. Give a firm, "No." He'll soon catch on. Remember, the entire family must take part. Each time you allow your dog to jump up you go back a step in training.

Biting

All puppies bite and try to chew on your fingers, toes, arms, etc. This is the time to teach them to be gentle and not to bite hard. Put your fingers in your puppy's mouth, and if he bites too hard then say "easy" and let him know he's hurting you. Squeal and act like you have been seriously hurt. If the puppy plays too rough and doesn't respond to your corrections, then he needs "time out" in his crate. You should be particularly careful with young children and puppies that still have their deciduous (baby) teeth. Those teeth are like needles and can leave little scars on youngsters.

Puppies and even adult dogs can get into mischief if they are bored. Providing your Berner with adequate daily exercise will keep him stimulated and out of trouble.

Biting in the more mature dog is something that should be prevented at all costs. If it occurs, quickly let him know in no uncertain terms that biting will not be tolerated. When biting is directed toward another dog (dog fight), don't get in the middle of it. Some authorities recommend breaking up a fight by elevating the hind legs. This would only be possible if there was a person to handle each dog. Obviously, it would be hard to fight with the hind legs off the ground. A dog bite is serious and should be given attention. Wash the bite with soap and water and contact your doctor. It is important to know the status of the offender's rabies vaccination.

Your dog must know who is boss. When biting occurs, you should seek professional help at once. On the other hand, you must not let your dog intimidate you and be so afraid of a bite that you can't discipline him. Professional help through your veterinarian, dog trainer, and/or behaviorist can give you guidance.

Digging

Bored dogs release their frustrations through mischievous behavior such as digging. Dogs shouldn't be left unattended outside, even if they are in a fenced-in yard. Usually, the dog is sent to "jail" (the backyard) because the owner can't tolerate him in the house. The culprit feels socially deprived and needs to be included in the owner's life. The owner has neglected the dog's training. The dog has not developed into the companion we desire. If you are one of these owners, then perhaps it is possible for you to change. Give him another chance. Some owners object to their dogs' unkempt coat and doggy odor. See that he is groomed on a regular schedule and look into some training classes.

Submissive Urination

Submissive urination is not a housetraining problem. It can occur in all breeds and may be more prevalent in some. Usually, it occurs in puppies, but occasionally it occurs in older dogs and may be in response to physical praise. Try verbal praise or ignoring your dog until after he has had a chance to relieve himself. Scolding will only make the problem worse. Many dogs outgrow this problem.

Coprophagia

Also known as stool eating, coprophagia sometimes occurs without a cause. It may begin with boredom and then becomes a habit that is

The Bernese Mountain Dog needs ample room in which to move and exercise. If you can't provide him with the proper accommodations, such as a large, fenced-in area, you may want to reconsider your choice of breed.

hard to break. Your best remedy is to keep the puppy on a leash and keep the yard picked up, so he won't have an opportunity to get into trouble. Your veterinarian can dispense a medication that is put on the dog's food that makes the stool taste bitter. Of course, this will do little good if your dog cleans up after other dogs.

The Runaway

There is little excuse for a dog to run away, because dogs should never be off leash except when supervised in a fenced-in yard.

Many prospective owners want to purchase a female because they believe a male is inclined to roam. It is true that an intact male is inclined to roam, which is one of the reasons a male should be neutered. However, females will roam also, especially if they are in heat. Regardless, these dogs should never be given this opportunity. A few years ago one of our clients elected euthanasia for her elderly dog because he radiographically appeared to have an intestinal blockage. The veterinarian suggested it might be a corncob. She assured him that was not possible

Before purchasing a Bernese Mountain Dog, make sure that you research the breed and are aware of its characteristics and special needs. Berners enjoy the outdoors and thrive on having a job to perform.

because they hadn't had any. Apparently, he roamed and raided the neighbor's garbage, and you guessed it—he had a corncob blocking his intestines. Another dog raided the neighbor's garbage and died from toxins from the garbage.

To give the benefit of the doubt, perhaps your dog escapes or perhaps you are playing with your dog in the yard and he refuses to come when called. You now have a runaway. Help! The first thing to remember is when you finally do catch your naughty dog, you must not discipline him. The reasoning behind this is that it is quite possible there could be a repeat performance, and it would be nice if he would respond to your sweet command the next time you used the recall.

Always kneel down when trying to catch the runaway. Dogs are afraid of people standing over them. Also, it would be helpful to have a treat or a favorite toy to help entice him to your side. After that initial runaway experience, start practicing the recall with your dog. You can let him drag a long line (clothesline), and then randomly call him and reel him in. Let him touch you first. Reaching for the dog can frighten him. Each time he comes reward him with a treat, and, eventually, he should get the idea that this is a nice experience. The long line prevents him from really getting out of hand. At least with the long line you can step on it and stop him.

Food Guarding

If you see signs of your puppy guarding his food, you should take immediate steps to correct the problem. It is not fair to your puppy to feed him in a busy environment where children or other pets may interfere with his eating. This can be the cause of food guarding. Puppies should be fed in their crates where they do not feel threatened. Another advantage of this is that the puppy gets down to the business of eating and doesn't fool around. Perhaps you have seen possessiveness over the food bowl or his toys. Start by feeding him out of your hand, and teach him that it is okay for you to remove his food bowl or toys and that you most assuredly will return them to him. If your dog is truly a bad actor and intimidates you, try keeping him on leash and perhaps sit next to him making happy talk. At feeding time, make him work for his reward (his dinner) by doing some obedience command such as sit or down. Before your problem gets out of control, you should get professional help. If he is out of control over toys, perhaps you should dispose of them or at least put them away when young children are around.

Mischief and Misbehavior

All puppies and even some adult dogs will get into mischief at some time in their lives. You should start by "puppy proofing" your house. Even so, it is impossible to have a sterile environment. For instance, if you would be down to four walls and a floor, your dog could still chew a hole in the wall. What do you do? Remember puppies should never be left unsupervised, so let us go on to the trusted adult dog that has misbehaved. His behavior may be an attention getter. Dogs, and even children, are known to do mischief even though they know they will be punished. Your puppy/dog will benefit from more attention and new direction. He may benefit from a training class or by reinforcement of the obedience he has already learned. How about a daily walk? That could be a good outlet for your dog, time together, and exercise for both of you.

Separation Anxiety

Separation anxiety occurs when dogs feel distress or apprehension about being separated from their owners. One of the mistakes owners make is to set their dogs up for their departure. Some authorities recommend paying little attention to the pet for at least ten minutes before leaving, and for the first ten minutes after you arrive home. The dog isn't cued to the fact you are leaving, and if you keep it low key, he learns to accept it as a normal everyday occurrence. Those dogs that are used to being crated usually accept your departure. Dogs that are anxious may have a serious problem and wreak havoc on the house within a few minutes after your departure. You can try to acclimate your dog to the separation by leaving for just a few minutes at a time, and returning and rewarding him with a treat. Don't get too carried away. Plan on this process taking a long time. A behaviorist can set down a schedule for you. Those dogs that are insecure, such as ones obtained from a humane shelter or those that have changed homes, may present more of a problem.

Punishment

A puppy should learn that correction is sometimes necessary and should not question your authority. An older dog that has never received correction may retaliate. There may be a time for physical punishment, but this does not mean hitting the dog. Do not use newspapers, fly swatters, etc. One type of correction that is used by the mother dog when she corrects her puppies is to take the puppy by the

A great companion, the Bernese Mountain Dog is good natured, courageous, loyal, and gentle.

scruff and shake him *gently*. For the older, larger dog, you can grab the scruff, one hand on each side of his neck, and lift his legs off the ground. This is effective because dogs feel intimidated when their feet are off the ground. Timing is of the utmost importance when punishment is necessary. Depending on the degree of fault, you might want to reinforce punishment by ignoring your dog for 15 to 20 minutes. Whatever you do, do not overdo corrections or they will lose value.

The most important advice to you is to be aware of your dog's actions. Even so, remember dogs are dogs and will behave as such, even though we might like them to be perfect little people. You and your dog will become neurotic if you worry about every little indiscretion. When there is reason for concern—don't waste time. Seek guidance. Dogs are meant to be loved and enjoyed.

REFERENCES

Valerie O'Farrell. *Manual of Canine Behavior.* British Small Animal Veterinary Association.

Brian Kilcommons. *Good Owners, Great Dogs.* Warner Books.

RESOURCES

Bernese Mountain Dog Club of America, Inc.
Corresponding Secretary: Anne Copeland
PO Box 2675
Palatine, IL 60078-2675
www.bmdca.org
Email: myrequestmail@aol.com

American Kennel Club
Headquarters:
260 Madison Avenue
New York, NY 10016

Operations Center:
5580 Centerview Drive
Raleigh, NC 27606-3390

Customer Services:
Phone: (919) 233-9767
Fax: (919) 816-3627
www.akc.org

The Kennel Club
1 Clarges Street
London
W1J 8AB
Phone: 087 0606 6750
Fax: 020 7518 1058
www.the-kennel-club.org.uk

The Canadian Kennel Club
89 Skyway Avenue
Suite 100
Etobicoke, Ontario, Canada
M9W 6R4
Order Desk & Membership:
1-800-250-8040
Fax: (416) 675-6506
www.ckc.ca

The United Kennel Club, Inc.
100 E. Kilgore Road
Kalamazoo, MI 49002-5584
(616) 343-9020
www.ukcdogs.com

INDEX